SKI TOWN *Soups*

SIGNATURE SOUPS *from* WORLD CLASS SKI RESORTS

JENNIE IVERSON

SKI TOWN GROUP Ltd.

FIRST EDITION

18   17   16   15   14   8   7   6   5   4

Library of Congress: 2012910016

ISBN 13: 978-0-9857290-0-4

Manufactured in China by Pettit Network Inc.

For photography credits, see page 219.
Book Design and typesetting by James Monroe Design, LLC.

For information about special purchases or custom editions, please contact:
info@skitownsoups.com

Ski Town Group, Ltd.
2121 N. Frontage Road, W. #5
Vail, Colorado 81657

SkiTownSoups.com

Ski Town Soups is dedicated to Masters Hunter and Grant.
Remember that, although soup is typically meant to simmer, life is meant to boil!

CONTENTS

Chowders & Bisques

Stews & Chilies

Hearty Soups

CONTENTS
Listed by Ski Resort

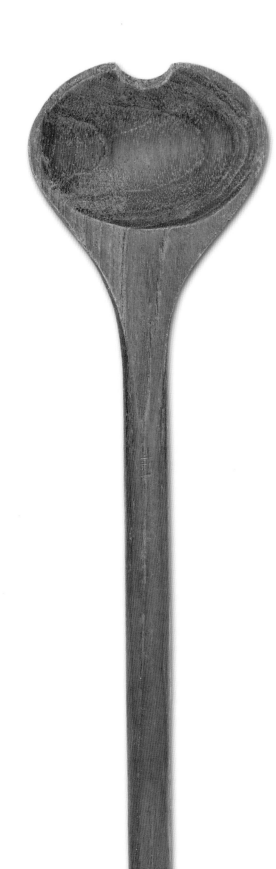

FOREWORD

It has been said that the mark of a great chef can be found in their creation of a great soup . . .

At my namesake restaurant in Vail, Colorado we source almost entirely local produce. This poses challenges living in a ski town that is under snow much of the year. This link with the seasons, including the anticipation of summer's first tomato, causes me to delight in Colorado and all it has to offer through the soups we create at the restaurant!

When I was nearing the end of my culinary studies at the Culinary Institute of America in Hyde Park, I seemed destined to live in a big city where many cutting edge restaurants were located. On September 11, 2001, I was working at a restaurant in Virginia, and a great client of mine died. All of a sudden, the importance of family and a strong community became a priority to me. I decided to return to Vail, Colorado, where my family has a home, and to the bustling ski town that had a vibrant, emerging culinary scene.

My husband and I opened Restaurant Kelly Liken in the spring of 2004 and quickly began establishing relationships with farmers, ranchers, and most importantly, with the members of our mountain community. We soon realized that the best way to make a lasting positive impact on our community was to start with the kids! We began to focus our philanthropic efforts primarily on the children in our community. Of course, my husband and I feed people for a living, so it became important for us to teach these children exactly where

their food comes from. Two years ago, these efforts grew into a program called Sowing Seeds and included greenhouses and outdoor-raised beds in two schools in Eagle County (with more on the way). This program has an amazing impact on the way these students learn and eat. Our director, Sandy Story, devised a curriculum that enables teachers to compliment classroom work with a daily portion of study inside the greenhouse. Today, not only do these students know where their food comes from, they also eat the produce that they grew in the greenhouse in the cafeteria!

We have seen our little home-grown project have a big impact. Our community is now pushing for a district-wide program called Fresh Approach which is designed to revamp our cafeterias and enable cooking from scratch in every school cafeteria in Eagle County. We are proud to live in the Eagle Valley, where the community has warmly embraced our family and supported our restaurant, and we are even more proud to be able to invest in the future of our community through its children. With each *Ski Town Soups* cookbook sold, a portion of the proceeds will go directly toward funding the Sowing Seeds program. Thank you for contributing to the future of our community's children.

Live In Season!
Kelly Liken

Ski Town Soups Background

The *Ski Town Soups* cookbook takes an individual's passion for soup and turns it into a must-have souvenir for skiers and foodies alike. A beautiful, colorful visual expression of ski towns, restaurant dining rooms, and unique soup recipes with ultimate regional flare, this cookbook will delight all winter enthusiasts! If you have spent time in a mountain village, then you have experienced the culinary scene and the amazing food the chefs prepare for ravenous skiers after mountain activities. Many of the flavor profiles in this cookbook originate from fresh and locally-sourced ingredients, which are very close to the hearts of those that contributed to this book. We hope that you will agree that a perfectly balanced recipe for life is a ski town, a comfortable restaurant, and a yummy bowl of soup!

Winning Restaurants Determined

In choosing the restaurants that are featured in this book, our company—Ski Town Group, Ltd.—designed and conducted a voting process to determine the "best" soup restaurants. We generated and contacted a large and random sample of hotel/resort/personal concierges and the local Chambers of Commerce in the surrounding communities. For select ski communities, we also interviewed a random selection of tourists. Primarily, we asked where their "best soup experiences" have been. Additionally, we conducted an extensive online search of restaurant reviews and recommendations. Based on the research results, the *Ski Town Soups* cookbook features chef-chosen soup recipes from the most beloved restaurants in world-class North American ski towns. The highlighted restaurants range from fine-dining to deli-style, and they are either located in the same ski town as the ski resort, or relatively close to the ski resort named.

Cookbook Usability

The cookbook is divided into 4 sections, by soup type: Pureed Soups, Chowders & Bisques, Stews & Chilies, and Hearty Soups. For easy reference, there are 2 types of Tables of Contents: 1—by soup recipe and 2—by ski resort. This usability appeals to travelers, foodies, skiers and home cooks!

"Difficulty Levels" within the Recipes

Each recipe is rated with a "difficulty level" that should be very familiar to winter enthusiasts! The green circle indicates a relatively easy recipe, with the ability to make the soup within 30–60 minutes and, often, using only one pot. The blue square is a bit more difficult, an intermediate level. This should be within most home cooks capabilities. The black diamonds are the most advanced recipes in this cookbook, and may challenge even the most adept home cook. Have fun with this! It's not a scientific rating system; the levels of difficulty were merely estimated by amount of time to complete the recipe and number and availability of the ingredients.

Recipe for Life

Visit **SkiTownSoups.com** for more information on chefs, restaurants and numerous food events throughout ski country to create a perfectly balanced recipe for life: a ski town, a comfortable restaurant, and a yummy bowl of soup!

For bonus soup recipes not found in this book, please visit **SkiSoup.com**

PUREED SOUPS

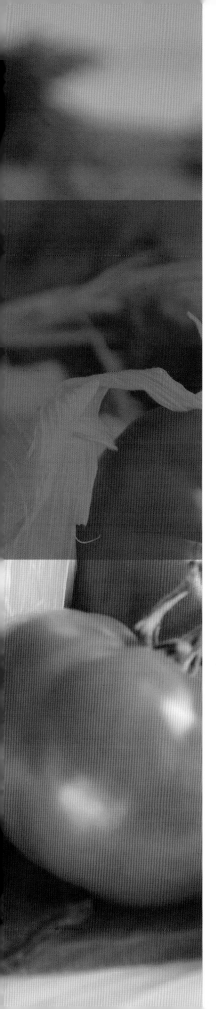

KABOCHA SQUASH SOUP

MANZANITA • CHEF TRACI DES JARDINS • TRUCKEE, CALIFORNIA

Combining her love of California and skiing, in 2009 Chef Traci Des Jardins opened Manzanita, her destination mountain restaurant in the Ritz-Carlton at Northstar in Lake Tahoe. Taking its name from the ubiquitous California tree, Manzanita offers Chef Des Jardins' signature French inspired California cuisine—with a regional mountain resort influence—sourcing organic, sustainable and locally grown meat and produce when possible.

2 Kabocha squash, peeled and chopped

2 onions, peeled and chopped

1 Thai chili, diced

4 oz. prosciutto scraps

1 Tbsp. Quatre Epice, available online or in specialty grocery stores

8 oz. Amaretto

1 quart cream

1 quart chicken stock

SERVES 4–6

In a stock pot, render prosciutto scraps. Add onions, squash and Thai chilies to prosciutto and rendered fat. Sweat for 20 minutes until squash is falling apart. Deglaze the pot with Amaretto and cook until dry. Add stock, cream and Quatre Epice.*

Cook for 25 minutes. In a blender or with an immersion blender, puree soup until smooth and silky.

* Quatre Epice is a simple mix of dried spices, often a mix of white pepper, nutmeg, cloves and ginger, but sometimes cinnamon and allspice are also used. The mixture is so often used by French cooks that it is called Quatre Epice in every language.

ALMOND COOKIE

½ cup sugar

¼ cup flour

½ tsp. almond extract

1 lb. butter

Whip butter and sugar in a standing mixer until completely aerated. Add flour and almond extract. Form in a large, flat round. Chill in refrigerator until ready for baking. Bake at 350 degrees for 10 minutes until golden brown. Cool and chop.

AMARETTO CREAM

8 oz. cream

3 oz. Amaretto

In a small saucepan, heat and reduce Amaretto until all alcohol is burned off. In a bowl, whip cream until stiff and add reduced Amaretto.

SERVING SUGGESTION:
Garnish this soup with almond cookie croutons and Amaretto cream.

CHILLED BEET SOUP

THE WILDFLOWER RESTAURANT • CHEF JACK HEYWOOD • SNOWBIRD, UTAH

The Wildflower Restaurant is located on the 3rd level of The Iron Blosam Lodge, at Snowbird Ski and Summer Resort. Sun-drenched flavors of Italy infuse the food and complement the mood at this casual romantic restaurant that touts "Intimate Italian" cuisine.

8 medium beets, peeled and chopped

4 large red onions, peeled and chopped

5 potatoes, peeled and chopped

1 cup garlic cloves, minced

Olive oil

½ quart heavy cream

⅔ cup rice vinegar

Salt and pepper to taste

SERVES 10–12

EASIEST

On low-medium heat, sweat beets, onions, potatoes, and garlic in a large, covered pot with a small amount of olive oil until caramelized. Add water until beets are covered. Boil for 5 minutes, then lower heat and simmer for 1½ hours.

Puree in a blender or with an immersion blender. Add heavy cream and rice vinegar. Season with salt and pepper to taste, then chill.

GOAT CHEESE GARNISH

Whip buttermilk and Sheppard's goat cheese until a smooth texture is reached.

SERVING SUGGESTION:
Serve Chilled Beet Soup with Goat Cheese Garnish, using a squeeze bottle to decorate the top of the soup.

ROASTED WINTER SQUASH SOUP

JACKSON FORK INN • HUNTSVILLE, UTAH

Only minutes away from Snowbasin and located in the Upper Ogden Valley, Jackson Fork Inn offers lodging and dining in their historic rare "Gambrel Roofed Dairy Barn". The name "Jackson Fork" comes from a large Jackson Hay Fork, made by the Jackson Farm Implement Co. The Jackson Fork Inn restaurant shows off beautiful knotty pine and early period antiques, along with excellent food prepared to accommodate each guest's individual tastes.

1 squash (butternut, acorn, banana or Hubbard)

3 garlic heads

1 medium yam

2 quarts chicken broth

1 large onion, diced

3 carrots, peeled and sliced

¼ cup butter

1 Tbsp. dried basil (¼ cup freshly chopped)

Salt and pepper to taste

SERVES 4–6

EASIEST

Preheat oven to 350 degrees. Wash squash and cut in half, lengthwise. Remove seeds and place on a foil-lined cookie sheet, cut side down. Slice yam in half, and place cut side down on cookie sheet. Wrap garlic heads in foil. Roast all in oven for 60–90 minutes, until fork tender. Remove from oven and cool.

In a large stock pot, combine broth, onions and carrots. Cook until onions and carrots are tender, add roasted garlic by extracting the "meat" out of the skins. Add peeled yam and peeled squash to pot. Add butter and basil. Adjust seasoning to taste.

Puree small batches at a time in a blender, or with an immersion blender, until smooth.

SERVING SUGGESTION:
Serve this soup with freshly grated parmesan cheese and parsley.

IDAHO POTATO, BEER & CHEESE SOUP

BRANDING IRON GRILL • CHEF NACHO ORDUNO & CHEF CHRIS MISTAK • ALTA, WYOMING

This delicious spin on the traditional beer cheese soup is made with Deep Powder Pale Ale, which is brewed exclusively for Grand Targhee Resort by the local Grand Teton Brewing Company. Deep Powder is golden blonde in color with a crisp body, light malt sweetness, pleasantly smooth character and dry palate.

2 Tbsp. oil

1 large onion, diced

1 Tbsp. garlic, minced

1 quart chicken stock or base

12 oz. Grand Teton Deep Powder Ale
(or another pale/golden ale)

1¾ quart heavy cream

2 large Idaho russet potatoes, peeled
and diced

2 cups asiago cheese

2½ cups cheddar cheese

1 tsp. chili powder

1 lemon, juiced

Salt and pepper to taste

SERVES 6–8

Sweat onions and garlic in oil in a large pot until the onion becomes tender. Add chicken stock, beer, heavy cream and potatoes. Boil and reduce heat to simmer for approximately 40 minutes or until potatoes are tender. Stir occasionally to avoid scalding.

Once potatoes are tender, remove pot from heat and fold in cheeses. Puree in a blender or with an immersion blender until smooth (you may use a sieve or strainer if a more elegant and smooth presentation is desired).

Finish by adding lemon juice, chili powder and salt and pepper to taste.

SERVING SUGGESTION:

Top with diced chives, green onions or bacon and shredded cheese. Pair with a fresh local brew poured into a frosted glass to drink while making or eating the soup!

ROASTED APPLE & BUTTERNUT SQUASH SOUP

HARRISON'S RESTAURANT • CHEF CASEY CHRISTENSEN • STOWE, VERMONT

Located in the heart of historic Stowe Village, Harrison's Restaurant and Bar is the Kneale family's version of what dining-out should be: unpretentious, memorable and, most of all, fun. On the authentic barn board walls, you will see original historic photos of Stowe, from the Kneale family's 80 years of living and working in the Stowe area. At Harrison's, you're always among friends!

1 large butternut squash

8 granny smith apples

1 large white onion, peeled and diced

1 jumbo carrot, peeled and diced

½ Tbsp. garlic, roasted

¼ cup brandy

1 cup apple cider

1 quart vegetable stock

1 Tbsp. fresh sage

Pinch of clove

Pinch of ground cinnamon

Pinch of cayenne pepper

½ tsp. fresh ginger

¼ cup Calvados apple brandy

2 Tbsp. chives, diced

Extra virgin olive oil

Salt and pepper to taste

SERVES **6–8**

MORE DIFFICULT

Preheat oven to 375 degrees. Cut butternut squash in half and remove seeds. Lightly coat flesh with extra virgin olive oil, salt, and pepper. Place flesh side down and roast for 30 minutes or until squash is soft. Remove from oven and cool. Remove and discard skin.

Cut apples into quarters and remove pits. Lightly coat with extra virgin olive oil, salt, and pepper. Roast in same oven for about 10 minutes.

In a medium sauce pan, sweat onions and carrots until soft. Add roasted garlic, brandy, butternut squash and apples (reserve some roasted apples for garnish). Cover and simmer for 5 minutes. Add cider, stock, clove, cinnamon, cayenne pepper and ginger, then simmer for 20 minutes. Remove from heat.

Add fresh sage. Puree with immersion blender or in a blender. Return to pot. Simmer for 15 minutes. Add salt and pepper to taste, and finish with Calvados.

SERVING SUGGESTION:
Garnish soup with reserved and diced roasted apples and chives.

MUSHROOM SOUP

SNAKE RIVER GRILL • CHEF JEFF DREW • JACKSON HOLE, WYOMING

Chef Jeff Drew has delighted patrons for over 10 years with modern American cuisine in the rustic elegance of the Snake River Grill. Chef Drew was nominated for "Best Chef: Northwest" at the 2010 James Beard Awards—the country's most coveted honor for chefs and restaurants.

⅛ lb. butter

¼ gallon crimini mushrooms and stems, finely chopped

⅓ cup parsnips, peeled and chopped

½ cup roasted shallots, peeled and coarsely chopped

⅓ gallon chicken stock

⅛ each chipotle chili, diced

⅝ Tbsp. garlic, roasted and pureed

¼ Tbsp. ground fennel seeds

⅓ Tbsp. kosher salt

⅓ cup sherry

¼ Tbsp. ground black pepper

⅜ Tbsp. porcini powder

⅓ Tbsp. chopped rosemary

SERVES 4

 MORE DIFFICULT

In a medium stock pot, melt butter. Add salt and half of the mushrooms; cook over medium-high heat. Cook mushrooms until browned; add remaining mushrooms and continue to cook until dark brown. Reduce heat to medium and add garlic, fennel and shallots; cook for 5 minutes. Stir often.

Add 1 cup chicken stock and scrape bottom of pot. Add sherry and parsnips; cook for only 1 minute. Add remaining stock and all remaining ingredients. Simmer for 30 minutes. Puree in a blender or with an immersion blender and strain through small-hole china cap. Adjust seasonings.

SERVING SUGGESTION:
If desired, garnish with a sprig of rosemary for visual appeal.

SPICED RUM SPIKED ACORN SQUASH SOUP
with Gorgonzola and Toasted Pecans

KELLY LIKEN • CHEF KELLY LIKEN • VAIL, COLORADO

Chef Kelly Liken is a 3-time James Beard nominee for Best Chef: Southwest (2009, 2010 and 2011). Chef Liken has garnered national recognition for her creativity in the kitchen, as well as her commitment and passion for her craft. She was featured in Bon Appétit, 2008 "Women Chefs: The Next Generation," as one of the emerging female chefs to watch in the United States, and has competed in the Food Network's Iron Chef America, as well as on Bravo's Season 7 of Top Chef D.C.

6 acorn squash, halved and seeded

1 medium yellow onion, roughly chopped

4 garlic cloves, smashed

1 large carrot, roughly chopped

1 thyme sprig

½ cup spiced rum

3 quarts vegetable broth

1 Tbsp. toasted pumpkin seed oil

4 Tbsp. pecan pieces, toasted

4 Tbsp. gorgonzola cheese, crumbled

Chopped chives for garnish

2 Tbsp. olive oil

Salt, pepper and cayenne to taste

SERVES 6

MORE DIFFICULT

Brush acorn squash with olive oil and season with salt and pepper. Roast, cut side down, on a baking sheet at 350 degrees until tender, about 30–40 minutes. In a large sauce pan, heat olive oil over medium heat. Add the onions, garlic, carrots and thyme sprig. Sweat until translucent.

Scrape the soft squash away from its skin and add to the sauce pot. Deglaze the pot with rum and reduce almost completely. Add vegetable broth and simmer approximately 30 minutes. Transfer to a blender and carefully puree the soup. Adjust seasoning with salt, pepper and a dash of cayenne.

SERVING SUGGESTION:
Divide the soup among 6 bowls and sprinkle with pecans, gorgonzola, chives and pumpkin seed oil before serving.

ROASTED RED PEPPER, TOMATO & BASIL SOUP

GREEN GODDESS CAFÉ • STOWE, VERMONT

Co-owner, Athena Scheidet says, "We're most proud of our soups. I've had well-traveled people say, 'This is the best soup I've had in my life.'" The soup menu at the Green Goddess Café changes daily, with offerings ranging from a Maryland Crab Chowder to a Curried Chicken Stew.

12 San Marzano tomatoes, blanched, peeled and diced, reserve juice

1 Vidalia onion, diced

3 medium carrots, peeled and diced

2 medium red peppers, char-roasted, peeled and chopped

3 garlic cloves, diced

4 cups chicken stock

1 cup fresh basil, chopped

1½ cups heavy cream

3 tsp. canola oil

Salt and pepper to taste

SERVES 4–6

EASIEST

In a sauce pan, heat oil and add onions and carrots. Cook until tender without browning, and then add garlic until softened. Add chicken stock, tomatoes, basil, red peppers and simmer on medium-low heat for 15 minutes. Remove from heat and blend, using an immersion blender until smooth consistency. Slowly add cream while stirring. Do not blend again. Salt and pepper to taste.

SERVING SUGGESTION:
If desired, garnish with a fresh basil leaf or 2.

GREEN PEA SOUP

COLLINS GRILL AT WATSON SHELTER • ALTA, UTAH

Collins Grill, a full-service, European mountain bistro/grill, is located mid-mountain of Collins Gulch, on the 3rd floor of the Watson Shelter. Ingredients are sourced locally and are as sustainable as possible in this dining location among the Wasatch Mountains at 9300 feet. Collins Grill supports Slow Food Utah, a local, Salt Lake City-based chapter of Slow Food USA. Slow Food USA is a global, grassroots movement linking the pleasure of food with a commitment to community and the environment, making the connection from "Plate to Planet."

2 lbs. peas, thawed

1 scallion bunch, sliced

½ cup fresh mint, chopped

2 Tbsp. olive oil

1 lemon, juiced

1 tsp. sambal

4 oz. crème fraîche

SERVES 6

Boil water in a stock pot and blanch peas, scallions, and mint for 30 seconds. Remove and place greens in an ice water bath. Puree greens with remaining ingredients and strain through a fine-mesh strainer. Heat to serving temperature.

SERVING SUGGESTION:
Garnish with pea shoots, herbed cream, or a selection of your favorite herbs (diced scallions, chives, and/or mint).

WHITE BEAN PANCETTA & CHIPOTLE GARLIC BLACK BEAN YIN & YANG SOUP

ZOOM • CHEF ROGER LAWS • PARK CITY, UTAH

Zoom, a Sundance Resorts restaurant located in Park City, delights guests with hints of the Southwest as well as the Far East. Chef Roger Laws, formerly of Zoom, could be described as an eclectic blend of International Influences and Rocky Mountain Fine Dining. His attention to texture and presentation is quite evident in this uniquely presented soup.

1 Tbsp. olive oil

2 Tbsp. butter

1 medium white onion, diced

1 celery stalk, diced

1 small carrot, diced

1 tsp. garlic, chopped

1 tsp. kosher salt

1 tsp. black pepper, coarsely ground

1½ cups pancetta, diced (or bacon, if pancetta is unavailable)

1 Tbsp. fresh sage, chopped

½ cup white balsamic vinegar

4 cups chicken stock

8 cups cooked white beans, in liquid (or canned beans, if necessary)

4 cups heavy cream

SERVES 8–10

White Bean Pancetta

MOST DIFFICULT

For both soups, soak dry beans in water overnight, then cook in lightly salted water on medium-high heat until beans soak up enough water to be soft, but not falling apart. Drain excess water and cool. If canned beans are used, skip this step.

Add olive oil to an 8-quart pot on medium heat. Add onions, garlic, celery, pancetta and carrots. Sauté until vegetables are soft and pancetta is cooked, but not quite crispy. Add butter, salt, pepper, sage and white balsamic vinegar; simmer for 5 minutes. Add stock, white beans in liquid, and heavy cream. Reduce to low heat and simmer for 45 minutes. Cool and puree in a blender or with an immersion blender.

1 Tbsp. olive oil

2 Tbsp. butter

1 medium red onion, diced

1 small carrot, diced

1 celery stalk, diced

2 Tbsp. garlic, chopped

1 tsp. kosher salt

1 tsp. black pepper, coarsely ground

1½ cups roasted red bell pepper

4 cups chicken stock

10 cups black beans, in liquid (or canned beans, if necessary)

1 Tbsp. cumin

¼ cup chipotle in adobo sauce, pureed

SERVES 8–10

Chipotle Garlic Black Bean

Add olive oil to an 8-quart pot on medium heat. Add onions, celery, carrots and garlic. Sauté until vegetables are soft. Add salt, pepper, roasted red pepper, cumin, chipotle puree and butter. Simmer for 5 minutes. Add stock and black beans in liquid. Reduce to low heat and simmer for 45 minutes. Cool and puree in a blender or with an immersion blender.

To plate the Yin and Yang, take a 10-inch section of aluminum foil and fold to create a 10-inch wide x 2-inch tall heavy gauge foil strip. In the soup bowl, place two ramekins, glasses or any cylindrical-shaped items that you can fit in the bowl side-by-side and run the foil strip between them. Bend one side of the strip around one cylinder to the left and the other to the right around the other cylinder to form an S shape. Remove the cylinders and leave the S shaped foil in the bowl, certain that it is flush to the bottom of the bowl.

Pour heated soups into separate pitchers. Using the foil as a separator, pour the soups in the bowl at the same time, slowly, on either side of the foil. Remove foil. Use a spoon and place a dab of white soup in black soup and vice versa for the eyes.

SERVING SUGGESTION:
For an added touch of color, make a bright red pepper or sundried tomato crème fraiche and trace the curve between the two soups.

EAST INDIAN SPINACH SOUP

THE BLONDE BEAR TAVERN • CHEF JOSEPH WREDE • TAOS SKI VALLEY, NEW MEXICO

At The Blonde Bear Tavern, this vegan soup was enjoyed by the late, great Taos artist, R.C. Gorman, a Navajo, great diner and friend of Taos restaurateurs. The Blonde Bear Tavern is located in the Edelweiss Lodge and Spa in Taos Ski Valley.

8 cups water

2 Tbsp. salt

1 lb. spinach, cleaned

4 Tbsp. unsalted butter

1 large onion, chopped

2 garlic cloves, minced

⅛ tsp. nutmeg

1 quart water

1 cup jasmine rice, cooked

4 Tbsp. salt

S ERVES 4 – 6

EASIEST

In a soup pot, boil 8 cups water and 2 Tbsp. salt. Blanch spinach in boiling water for 2 minutes. Drain and set spinach aside. Clean (or use another soup pot), and heat on medium. Melt butter and add onions and garlic, stirring until onions are translucent. Add spinach, nutmeg, cooked rice and water; simmer for 15 minutes. Puree soup in blender, or use an immersion blender to create a fine puree. Salt to taste, approximately 4 Tbsp.

SERVING SUGGESTION:

This wonderfully healthy soup, which will reenergize the body, doesn't need any accompaniments.

CURRY CARROT SOUP

THE BLONDE BEAR TAVERN • CHEF JOSEPH WREDE • TAOS SKI VALLEY, NEW MEXICO

Carrots are sweet! However, the longer the distance a carrot has to travel to the kitchen, the more its starch develops. Chef Joseph Wrede highly recommends using local carrots—the Curry Carrot Soup will benefit by the natural and local quality of the well-handled, not well-traveled, local vegetable.

2 lbs. carrots, peeled and sliced

4 Tbsp. unsalted butter

3 Tbsp. yellow curry

3 Tbsp. Madeira

3 fresh thyme sprigs, picked and stemmed

5 cups chicken stock

1 cup cream

Salt to taste

SERVES 4–6

EASIEST

In a sauce pan, toast yellow curry over medium heat for 3 minutes. Remove from heat and set aside.

In a separate sauce pan, simmer cream and reduce by half, over medium heat for 12 minutes. Remove from heat and set aside.

In a soup pot over medium-high heat, melt butter and add carrots, stir. After sautéing, deglaze carrots for 5 minutes with Madeira. Add thyme, toasted curry and chicken stock. Reduce heat to medium and cook for 20 minutes. Add reduced cream and puree in a blender or with an immersion blender. Adjust seasoning with salt to taste.

SERVING SUGGESTION:
Fresh and pure, serve this sweet puree unadorned.

CREAMY ROASTED RED PEPPER
with Arugula & Great Northern Beans

CB (COVERED BRIDGE) GRILLE • CHEF ADAM JESS • COPPER MOUNTAIN, COLORADO

This signature evening soup is from CB Grille—a restaurant that uses locally-sourced proteins and fresh vegetables combined with a wood-fired grill to create an inspired, creative and unique dining experience. Chef Adam Jess, the creative force since CB Grille opened in 2006, features nightly soups that are legendary at Copper Mountain. Homeowners, day-guests and employees all rave about his kettle creations!

1 cup yellow onion, chopped

2 Tbsp. garlic, chopped

¼ cup tomato paste

2 cups white wine

3 quarts heavy cream

3 cups roasted red peppers

2 bay leaves

1 Tbsp. dried tarragon

1 Tbsp. dried thyme

2 Tbsp. coriander

1 Tbsp. dry mustard

3 Tbsp. fresh parsley

¼ cup flour

¼ cup butter

2 Tbsp. white balsamic vinegar

3 cups great northern beans

4 cups arugula, chopped

Salt and pepper to taste

Goat cheese, crumbled

Fresh croutons

SERVES 10–12

 MORE DIFFICULT

In a large stock pot over medium heat, sauté onions and garlic until softened. Add tomato paste and cook until caramelized. Add wine and deglaze the pot by stirring with a wooden spoon. Add cream, peppers and all herbs. Boil and reduce heat to a simmer for approximately 30 minutes.

Remove bay leaves. Puree soup in a blender or with an immersion blender until smooth. Return mixture to the stock pot.

In a separate skillet, make a roux: combine flour and butter; stir until completely mixed. Cook for 5 minutes. Whisk small amounts of roux into pureed mixture, approximately 2 Tbsp. Add vinegar, beans, and arugula to soup. Boil and reduce heat to a simmer. Cook for approximately 1 hour. Adjust seasonings to taste.

SERVING SUGGESTION:
Ladle into a soup bowl and garnish with crumbled goat cheese and fresh croutons.

BUTTERNUT SQUASH SOUP

BIG SKY RESORT • CHEF DON GRIFFIN • BIG SKY, MONTANA

"Montana skiing has arrived!" SKI Magazine *announced in its September 1973 issue. Now, decades later, Big Sky Resort is home to the "Biggest Skiing in America" and known as one of the best ski resorts in the nation. Big Sky Resort continues to set standards for skiing in Montana—and in the Rockies—with un-crowded slopes and non-existent lift lines.*

3 Tbsp. butter

¾ cup onions, chopped

2 lbs. butternut squash, peeled, halved, seeded and cut into 1-inch chunks

1 medium green apple, cored and cut into 1-inch chunks

½ cup pecans, chopped and toasted

1 Tbsp. brandy (optional)

⅓ cup orange juice

½ tsp. ground ginger

¼ tsp. ground nutmeg

¾ cup heavy cream

1¾ cups chicken or vegetable stock

Sour cream (optional)

SERVES 4–6

In a large saucepan, melt butter on low-to-medium heat. Add onions; cook and stir for 3 minutes or until slightly softened. Add squash, apples, and pecans. Add brandy, if desired. Cook on medium heat for 1 minute, stirring occasionally.

Stir in orange juice, ginger, nutmeg and stock. Boil and reduce heat to low; cover and simmer for 25 minutes or until squash is tender. Stir occasionally.

Cool slightly. Puree soup in batches in blender on high speed, or with an immersion blender, until smooth. Return to sauce pan. Stir in heavy cream. Cook until heated through.

SERVING SUGGESTION:
Ladle into soup bowls and top each serving with a dollop of sour cream.

MUSHROOM SOUP
with Ramp Leaf & Truffle Pistou

MICHAEL'S ON THE HILL RESTAURANT • CHEF MICHAEL KLOETI • WATERBURY CENTER, VERMONT

Michael's on the Hill is located in a circa-1820 farmhouse, surrounded by acres of rolling lawns, forest and perennial gardens. Spectacular views of the Green Mountains and sunsets make Michael's a popular stop for photographers and tourists alike. Owners Michael and Laura Kloeti were awarded Vermont Restaurateurs of the Year in 2011. They continue to respect the entire farm-to-table process—the producers' pride in their food and the environment which they use with care. It's no wonder USA Today wrote, "Laura and Michael Kloeti were among the first chef/restaurateurs to champion local ingredients...and they've been joined by a handful of other chefs whose restaurants are committed to showcasing Vermont's bounty."

1 lb. crimini mushrooms, sliced

1 cup porcini mushrooms, dried

1 medium yellow onion, peeled and diced

6 cups vegetable broth

¾ cup Arborio rice

10 oz. heavy cream

Salt and freshly ground black pepper to taste

Water to cover dried mushrooms

SERVES 8

Cover dried porcini mushrooms with warm water. Rehydrate, then strain and reserve both water and mushrooms. In a stock pot, sauté onions until they become translucent. Add crimini mushrooms and sauté until liquid is drawn out. Add rehydrated mushrooms, broth and porcini liquid, then simmer.

Add rice to pot and cook until completely tender. Blend and strain. Add cream and season to taste.

ROASTED MUSHROOMS

½ lb. crimini mushrooms, quartered

½ lb. oyster mushrooms, de-stemmed

½ lb. shitake mushrooms, de-stemmed and quartered

2 Tbsp. extra virgin olive oil

1 Tbsp. mixed herbs

½ tsp. salt

Freshly ground black pepper to taste

Preheat oven to 400 degrees and gently toss all ingredients together. Spread evenly on a sheet pan and roast for 15 minutes. Stir mushrooms and roast for an additional 15–20 minutes until golden brown.

RAMP LEAF AND TRUFFLE PISTOU

1 oz. (4 leaves) ramp leaves, washed

1½ tsp. black truffles, chopped

¼ lemon, juiced

¼ cup extra virgin olive oil

¼ cup white truffle oil

¼ tsp. salt

Freshly ground black pepper to taste

Place all ingredients in a food processor and blend until just chopped and incorporated. If you prefer, you may incorporate ingredients by using a mortar and pestle.

SERVING SUGGESTION: Ladle soup into a bowl, top with roasted mushrooms and drizzle with pistou. For an extra decadent touch, top with shaved truffles.

SHERRY & CHESTNUT SOUP
with Celery Root & Fennel Pollen

EASTSIDE BISTRO • CHEF KALON WALL • CRESTED BUTTE, COLORADO

EastSide Bistro offers a breathtaking backdrop of Mt. Crested Butte in a warm, intimate and beautifully decorated dining room. Owners Ben and Liz Satterlee, along with Chef Kalon Wall, create seasonal menus that reflect locally-sourced baked goods and farm-fresh produce.

2 shallots, chopped

1 onion, chopped

4 celery stalks, chopped

3 garlic cloves, sliced

2 cups chestnuts, peeled and roasted

1 potato, thinly sliced

4 cups dry sherry

4 cups vegetable stock

1 cup cream

2 Tbsp. butter

¼ cup + 1 Tbsp. olive oil

Salt and pepper to taste

SERVES 6–8

In a sauce pot with ¼ cup olive oil and butter, combine shallots, onions, celery and garlic with a pinch of salt, then heat until translucent. Add chestnuts and potato; continue to sauté until lightly caramelized. Deglaze with sherry and reduce by half.

Add vegetable stock and simmer until vegetables are soft. Add cream. Puree mixture in a blender or with an immersion blender until silky smooth. Season with salt and pepper to taste.

SERVING SUGGESTION:
Garnish with fennel pollen, olive oil drizzle, chopped chervil and brunoise (small ⅛-inch dice) celery root, which has been lightly sautéed in butter and kept warm.

TRUFFLED CELERIAC SOUP

LUNA BISTRO AT STRATTON MOUNTAIN CLUB • CHEF PAUL KROPP • STRATTON MOUNTAIN, VERMONT

Executive Chef Paul Kropp creates casual and fine dining for Stratton Mountain Club, which includes the featured Luna Bistro. This private alpine club is located at the base of Stratton Mountain, adjacent to the gondola.

1 sweet onion, cleaned and diced

2 garlic cloves, diced

1 Tbsp. butter

2 Tbsp. extra virgin olive oil

1½ lbs. potatoes, cleaned and roughly diced

3 lbs. celeriac root, cleaned and roughly diced

1 quart chicken stock

2–4 thyme sprigs, tied

½ cup heavy cream

Pinch of sea salt

2–3 twists of black pepper

SERVES 4–6

 MORE DIFFICULT

In a stock pot, sweat onions and garlic with butter and olive oil until translucent. Add potatoes, celeriac root, thyme and chicken stock. Boil and reduce heat to simmer until vegetables are tender. Add heavy cream and cook until slightly thickened. Remove thyme and adjust seasoning. Puree in a blender or with an immersion blender. Strain for a smoother consistency, if desired.

TRUFFLE OIL

¼ cup extra virgin olive oil

1 Tbsp. black truffle, diced

Puree extra virgin olive oil with black truffle.

TRUFFLE CRÈME FRAICHE

¼ cup crème fraiche

Pinch of sea salt

1 Tbsp. black truffle, diced

Sea salt and pepper to taste

Whip crème fraiche, salt, and black truffle. Add salt and pepper to taste.

SERVING SUGGESTION:

Ladle soup into bowls, drizzle with truffle oil and place a small amount of the truffle crème fraiche mixture in the middle. Top with micro greens.

THAI SPICED WINTER SQUASH SOUP

RUPERT'S AT HOTEL MCCALL • CHEF GARY KUCY • MCCALL, IDAHO

This gluten-free soup is a favorite at Rupert's! The winter squash is sourced locally from Appleton Farms in Council, Idaho, but you may try different types of squash to find one that best suits your taste: Red Kuri, Kabocha or Butternut are good choices. This recipe is a wonderful example of how Chef Gary Kucy built his diverse career by incorporating culinary traditions from around the world. Along with delicious food, Rupert's features lakeside dining with spectacular views and is located in the historic Hotel McCall, the oldest hotel in McCall, Idaho.

1½ lbs. winter squash, peeled, seeded and chopped

3 Tbsp. canola oil

4 shallots, thinly sliced

2 garlic cloves, finely chopped

3 Tbsp. ginger, freshly chopped

2 tsp. ground coriander

1 tsp. ground cumin

1 Tbsp. yellow Thai curry paste

2 quarts vegetable or shrimp stock

¼ cup honey

2 limes, juiced

Serves 4–6

 EASIEST

Sauté garlic, shallots and ginger in canola oil over medium heat. Cook until softened, but not browned. Add curry paste, cumin and coriander. Cook for 2 minutes until aromatic. Add chopped squash and stock; simmer for 20 minutes until squash is soft. Remove from heat. Puree in a blender or with an immersion blender then strain through a fine sieve. Add honey and lime juice and adjust seasoning, if necessary.

SERVING SUGGESTION:

Thai Spiced Winter Squash Soup is an excellent neutral base to pair with grilled shrimp or peanut chicken.

CREAMY TOMATO BASIL SOUP

SIMPLY GOURMET • LAKE PLACID, NEW YORK

Simply Gourmet believes in using the freshest local and sustainable ingredients—without additives or preservatives. Family-owned-and-operated by Holly and Mickey Healy and Phoebe Burns, a diner can expect great ingredients, wonderful preparation and a beautiful presentation.

2 Tbsp. olive oil

4 Tbsp. butter

1 medium onion, diced

1 garlic clove, finely minced

28 oz. can diced tomatoes, unseasoned

½ cup fresh basil, diced

2 Tbsp. vegetable or beef base (no MSG,
like Better than Bouillon)

2 cups milk

2 cups heavy cream (or low fat milk)

Salt and pepper to taste

Croutons (optional)

Parmesan or cheddar cheese, grated

SERVES 4–6

In 4-quart saucepan, heat oil over medium heat. Add butter and when it bubbles, add onions and sauté until soft, about 5 minutes. Add garlic, tomatoes, ¼ cup basil and base. Simmer approximately 20 minutes until tomatoes are soft.

Puree in a blender (or with an immersion blender) until smooth. Return to pan. Add milk and cream and heat to serving temperature. Adjust seasoning. Add remaining basil.

SERVING SUGGESTION:

Top soup with croutons and sprinkle with grated cheeses. Accompany soup with Grown-Up Grilled Cheese: place brie and bacon between 2 slices of rustic sandwich bread and grill.

CREAM OF ROASTED POTATO
with Habanero, Leeks and Manchego Cheese

RELISH • CHEF MATTHEW FACKLER • BRECKENRIDGE, COLORADO

Chef and Owner Matthew Fackler, along with his wife, Lisa, have been Breckenridge locals for many years. And, with Relish, they are fulfilling a life-long culinary dream!

¼ cup butter

1 cup onions, diced

2 cups leeks, crescent-cuts

½ cup celery, diced

⅛ cup garlic, chopped

4 Yukon Gold potatoes

3 Idaho potatoes

2 oz. olive oil

¼ cup white wine

3 quarts chicken stock

1 quart heavy cream

¼ cup parsley, chopped

⅛ cup cilantro, chopped

½ habanero chili, seeded (or a pinch of habanero chili powder)

SERVES 6–8

Preheat oven to 400 degrees. Wash potatoes and cut into large chunks. Toss potatoes in olive oil and roast until caramelized and soft, approximately 30 minutes. Roast habanero chili with a kitchen torch.

Sweat diced vegetables (onions, leeks, celery and garlic) in butter until translucent. Deglaze with white wine, add chicken stock and habanero chili. Simmer and add roasted potatoes. Cook until potatoes are soft. Add cream and herbs.

In a blender, or with an immersion blender, puree until smooth.

SERVING SUGGESTION:
Serve this soup with grated manchego cheese or a cheese of your choice.

ROASTED TOMATO SOUP

BISTRO • CHEF JOHN MURCKO • PARK CITY, UTAH

Roasted Tomato Soup is courtesy of Chef John Murcko, formerly of Bistro and semifinalist for the 2012 James Beard Foundation Awards, the nation's most prestigious recognition program for professionals in the food and beverage industry. Bistro, the newest restaurant at Canyons Resort, serves gourmet "Modern American" cuisine in a Parisian-style intimate dining room. Bistro at Canyons is the nation's first kosher restaurant located in a ski resort.

2½ lbs. Roma tomatoes,
cut in half lengthwise

4 Tbsp. olive oil

1 medium onion, chopped

4 garlic cloves, minced

Dash of red pepper flakes

1 cup basil, freshly chopped

15 oz. can diced tomatoes

14 oz. can white beans, strained and rinsed

6 cups vegetable broth (or chicken broth)

Salt and pepper to taste

S ERVES 6–8

 EASIEST Preheat oven to 400 degrees. Spread tomatoes on a baking sheet and drizzle with 2 Tbsp. of olive oil. Season with salt and pepper and roast for approximately 45 minutes.

In a large stock pot, heat the other 2 Tbsp. of olive oil over medium heat. Add onions and cook until tender, about 2–3 minutes. Stir in garlic and red pepper flakes. Cook for another 2–3 minutes. Add canned tomatoes, canned beans, fresh basil and vegetable broth. Stir in the oven-roasted tomatoes. Cook for approximately 30 minutes over medium-low heat.

Use an immersion blender to puree the soup in the stock pot, or transfer soup to a food processor or blender to blend. The soup should be smooth, with a few tomato chunks. Season with salt and pepper to taste.

SERVING SUGGESTION:
Serve warm after a cold day on the mountain.

ROASTED SQUASH SOUP
with Whipped Maple & Fresno Chilies

TRUFFLE PIG • CHEF GEORGE MORRIS • STEAMBOAT SPRINGS, COLORADO

Truffle Pig features casually elegant cuisine crafted from the finest and freshest ingredients, including organic fruits and vegetables, free-range game and meats and line-caught seafood. Truffle Pig pairs the dishes with outstanding wines from around the region and the world. Whether a quick grab-and-go breakfast and coffee in the market, a slope-side lunch with friends, or a quiet romantic dinner and dessert by candlelight with that special someone, the Truffle Pig Restaurant is the place in Steamboat to escape winter and warm up with friendly folks.

1½ lbs. butternut squash

1½ lbs. blue hubbard squash

1 large carrot, peeled and thinly sliced

1 celery stalk, thinly sliced

1 large onion, peeled and thinly sliced

1 fresno chili with seeds, thinly sliced

2 garlic cloves, thinly sliced

1 oz. canola oil

4 oz. butter

1 cup white wine

3 cups chicken stock

1 cup heavy cream

Salt and pepper to taste

3 thyme sprigs, picked

1 fresno chili, sliced into rings

SERVES 6–8

Cut squashes in half, remove the seeds and pulp and season with salt and pepper. Place face down on an oiled sheet tray and roast in a 375 degree oven until tender, about 45 minutes. When squash is soft and tender, remove from oven, scoop out flesh and reserve.

Heat a large sauce pot over medium heat. Add butter and oil. When butter is completely melted, add uncooked vegetables. Reduce heat to low and slowly sweat vegetables until soft and translucent. Increase heat to medium and add white wine. Reduce wine by half and add chicken stock and squash. Boil and remove from heat.

Puree soup in a blender on high until smooth; this may be done in batches. Strain and whisk in the cream. Season with salt and pepper to taste.

WHIPPED MAPLE GARNISH:

1 cup maple syrup

¼ cup hot water

½ tsp. (3 grams) Versawhip 600K*, available online

Put water into a blender and blend at high speed. Add Versawhip 600K to dissolve. In a standing mixer with the whisk attachment, add maple syrup and Versawhip/water mixture. Mix on high for 10 minutes or until fluffy.

* Versawhip 600K is a natural ingredient based on dairy or vegetable proteins. It has exceptional whipping performance and produces very stable foams.

SERVING SUGGESTION:
Garnish desired soup bowl with a few dollops of Whipped Maple, some thyme leaves, and fresno chili rings.
Pour in the soup.

ACORN SQUASH SOUP
with Whitefish Caviar Crème Fraiche

CAFÉ KANDAHAR • CHEF ANDY BLANTON • WHITEFISH, MONTANA

Café Kandahar, located inside the Kandahar Lodge in the heart of the Whitefish Mountain village, has distinguished itself as a premier dining destination in Northwest Montana. Through its ongoing commitment and intuitive approach to remain creative in the ever-evolving culinary world, Café Kandahar is dedicated to providing guests with an exquisite and fascinating fine dining experience. Chef Blanton was a semifinalist for the James Beard Foundation Awards, "Best Chef: Northwest" in 2010. In 2012, he was selected as the first Montana chef to cook at the James Beard House in New York City.

2½ Tbsp. olive oil

2 acorn squash

1 yellow onion, diced

2 celery stalks, diced

3 assorted sweet peppers, diced

4 garlic cloves, minced

2 shallots, minced

2 bay leaves

4 thyme sprigs, tied with butcher twine or string

Pinch of cayenne

Pinch of nutmeg

Pinch of black pepper, freshly ground

2 tsp. kosher salt (if using a salted broth, decrease this amount)

½ cup white wine (optional)

½ gallon vegetable stock (or low-salt/unsalted broth or water)

1 quart heavy whipping cream

SERVES 6–8

MOST DIFFICULT

Preheat oven to 375 degrees. Cut squash in half lengthwise and remove seeds. Rub squash with 1 Tbsp. olive oil. Cut side down, place squash on baking sheet or roasting tray. Roast until cooked and soft to touch, about 45–60 minutes.

Heat 1 ½ Tbsp. olive oil in a medium saucepot on high heat until just smoking. Add onions, celery and peppers. Sauté until translucent, about 3–4 minutes, stirring constantly. Do not let vegetables brown. Reduce heat to medium, add garlic and shallots and continue to sauté for 1 minute. Add thyme, salt, black pepper, cayenne, nutmeg and bay leaves. Stir spices for about 30 seconds.

Add white wine, and reduce before adding vegetable stock (if no wine is used, pour in stock). Increase heat and boil. Reduce heat and simmer. While liquid is simmering, peel squash with your fingers or scoop the flesh out with a spoon. Add squash into simmering broth. Stir in heavy cream; return heat to high and boil, stirring often. Once boil is achieved, reduce heat and simmer. Remove bay leaves and thyme sprigs. Puree using a blender, immersion blender, or food processor. Adjust seasoning, if necessary.

WHITEFISH CAVIAR CRÈME FRAICHE

¼ cup sour cream

¼ cup heavy cream

Whitefish caviar

Salt and pepper to taste

Lemon juice to taste, freshly squeezed (optional)

Mix together heavy cream and sour cream. Let the mixture stand at room temperature for 3–4 hours. Add Whitefish Caviar. Season to taste with lemon juice, salt and pepper.

SERVING SUGGESTION:
Garnish each soup portion with Whitefish Caviar Crème Fraiche.

RED BELL PEPPER PARMESAN SOUP

UTE CITY • CHEF ROB MACCLANAHAN • ASPEN, COLORADO

Along Aspen's Restaurant Row, Ute City beckons all with its heady, rustic aromas and floor-to-ceiling windows framing views of Aspen Mountain. Inspired to recreate the old world ski-town charm of Aspen, local restaurateur, Walt Harris created this upscale local hangout with great food at affordable prices. Chef Rob MacClanahan shares his coveted Red Bell Pepper Parmesan Soup recipe, which claimed the Aspen Annual Soupsköl trophy for 2012.

7–8 lbs. red bell pepper, chopped

¼ lb. butter

3 large yellow onions, chopped

4 Tbsp. garlic, chopped

4 cups parmesan, freshly grated

1 cup flour

1 cup oyster sauce

Salt and pepper to taste

2 quarts plus 2 cups duck stock (or chicken stock)

Serves 8–10

In a large stock pot, melt butter and sauté onions for approximately 5 minutes. Add garlic and cook for another 3–4 minutes. Add 2 cups stock and chopped peppers. Cover and simmer over medium heat for 15 minutes, stirring frequently.

Uncover and cook for another 15–20 minutes, allowing moisture to evaporate and reduce. Stir in flour and remaining stock; simmer and stir at a mild boil for 5 minutes.

Remove from heat. Puree in a blender or with an immersion blender. Strain through a china cap with a small hole. Add oyster sauce, cheese and seasonings. Stir until cheese has melted.

TURMERIC SOUR CREAM

1½ cups sour cream

2 tsp. Turmeric

Water to thin

Combine ingredients in a squeeze bottle. Design plated soup.

DUCK CONFIT GRILLED CHEESE

2 cups duck confit, roughly chopped

3 Tbsp. cream cheese

1 cup parmesan, freshly grated

Bread of your choice

Combine ingredients and thinly spread on bread slices. Grill the sandwich and cut into quarters or 2-inch squares.

SERVING SUGGESTION:
Garnish with Turmeric Sour Cream and Duck Confit Grilled Cheese.

BUTTERNUT SQUASH & APPLE SOUP

THE NARROWS AT SHORE LODGE • CHEF ERIC GRUBER • MCCALL, IDAHO

Chef Eric Gruber's philosophy of building menus around seasonal and regional ingredients is showcased most notably at The Narrows, Shore Lodge's fine dining restaurant. Shore Lodge, the quintessential mountain retreat, is nestled on the sandy, southern shores of glacier-carved Payette Lake, only 10 minutes from Brundage Mountain Resort.

2 large butternut squash

3 green apples, peeled, cored and diced

1 white onion, sliced

½ lb. brown sugar

½ cup brandy

1 gallon chicken stock

5 fresh sage leaves, minced

¼ lb. butter

½ Tbsp. chili powder

1 tsp. cayenne pepper

2 Tbsp. salt

1 Tbsp. white pepper

SERVES 6–8

EASIEST Preheat oven to 350 degrees. Cut squash in half lengthwise and remove seeds. Roast squash, cut-side down, on a baking sheet in oven for 30 minutes. Cool, remove and discard outer skin.

In a large stock pot over medium heat, sauté onions and apples until caramelized, about 15–20 minutes. Add butternut squash and brown sugar. Continue to cook 10 minutes. Add brandy and reduce until liquid has evaporated. Add chicken stock. Boil and reduce heat to a simmer. Add all remaining ingredients, except salt and peppers. Simmer for 30 minutes. Puree soup in a blender or with an immersion blender and season with salt and peppers.

SERVING SUGGESTION:
Garnish soup with a dollop of sour cream and a sprinkle of cinnamon.

John Murcko

Talisker Corporation's Executive Chef, John Murcko, previously brought more than 20 years of professional culinary experience to the Talisker Restaurant Collection, which includes signature restaurants Talisker on Main, The Farm, Bistro at Canyons and Slopes by Talisker. Originally from Holly, Michigan, Chef Murcko's fascination with fine cuisine began at age 10 when his father took him to New York's Tavern on the Green. Throughout his career, Murcko and his creations have been lauded in publications including The New York Times, Wine Spectator, Huffington Post, *SHAPE* Magazine, *Salt Lake Magazine*, *Salt Lake Tribune* and *City Weekly*.

For the second consecutive year, Talisker on Main was named "Best Restaurant in Park City." The magazine singled out Murcko for "reinventing" Park City as a dining destination. Not content to rest on his laurels, Murcko opened The Farm as part of the Canyons' ambitious resort enhancement project. One of nearly a dozen new dining venues at Canyons, The Farm was selected by *Salt Lake Magazine* as the "Best New Restaurant in Utah." The magazine applauded The Farm for sourcing the majority of its ingredients from within 200 miles of Park City, Utah.

In 2012, Chef John Murcko was named a semifinalist for the James Beard Foundation Award. Murcko said, "I'm humbled to be named alongside some of the best chefs in America by the James Beard Foundation."

See page 40 for Chef John Murcko's Roasted Tomato Soup.

Gary Kucy

Gary Kucy, Executive Chef of Rupert's at Hotel McCall in McCall, Idaho, is fast establishing himself as a notable and rising star in the culinary world. Rupert's is excited to bring Gary's passion for all things food to guests each evening!

Chef Gary Kucy has built his diverse career incorporating culinary traditions from around the world. Gary's culinary training began with a prestigious four-year formal apprenticeship at the five-star, five-diamond Arizona Biltmore Resort in Phoenix, Arizona. Gary then moved to work with Mark Miller at the Coyote Café in Santa Fe, New Mexico, where he spent eight years assisting in opening restaurants, writing cookbooks, and promoting southwestern cuisine worldwide. His work included cooking stints in Singapore, Mexico, Los Angeles, San Francisco, Philadelphia, New York and Seattle. He subsequently spent two years as chef at the Snake River Grill, an upscale fine dining restaurant in the heart of Jackson, Wyoming. In December 2005, he opened and became Executive Chef of Tamarack Resort's premier restaurant, Morels.

His culinary inspiration has been enhanced by numerous international culinary tours, including visits to more than 25 countries, where he explored, tasted and researched local cuisine. Chef Gary's wife, Stacey Kucy, is an accomplished Pastry Chef, whose pastry creations are occasionally featured at Rupert's. Stacey is also the owner and operator of Stacey's Cakes in McCall, specializing in wedding cakes, pastries and special occasion desserts.

See page 35 for Chef Gary Kucy's Thai Spiced Winter Squash Soup. Also, visit SkiTownSoups.com for Chef Gary Kucy's Roasted Sweet Pepper Soup.

CHOWDERS
& BISQUES

ROASTED KABOCHA SQUASH BISQUE
with Ginger Essence

TASTINGS FOOD AND SPIRITS • CHEF JEFFREY WEISS • TROY, VERMONT

After stints in Europe, Hawaii, California and the Caribbean, Chef Jeffrey Weiss and his wife returned to his native Vermont and opened Tastings Food and Spirits featuring modern American comfort food. At Tastings, Chef Weiss is always changing the Vermont Fresh menu and specials, which are inspired by local and regional ingredients chosen at their peak for flavor and freshness! His cuisine is prepared and presented in a creative fashion and is always accompanied by the finest in Vermont hospitality.

1 Kabocha squash, halved and seeded

1 carrot, peeled and sliced

1 onion, peeled and chopped

2 celery stalks, chopped

1 Tbsp. ginger, freshly minced

1 lemongrass stalk, chopped

1 tsp. red curry paste

12 oz. coconut milk

1 quart water or vegetable stock

Salt and pepper to taste

SERVES 8

EASIEST

In a 350 degree oven, roast squash halves on an oiled sheet until tender. Remove flesh and place in a stock pot. Add all remaining ingredients and simmer for 45 minutes. Puree in a blender or with an immersion blender. Strain and adjust seasoning with salt and pepper to taste.

SERVING SUGGESTION:
Creamy and smooth, this bisque will warm your soul without any additions.

SMOKED TOMATO BISQUE
with Grilled Cheese Dipper

THE BLACKSMITH RESTAURANT • CHEF GAVIN MCMICHAEL • BEND, OREGON

Base community, Bend, Oregon, is a short distance from Mt Bachelor, which offers the most skiable acreage and highest resort peak in the Cascades. Located on the eastern flanks of Oregon's Central Cascades, Mt Bachelor has become famous for its consistently light and dry snow quality and variety of terrain, with 360 degree access off the 9,065 foot summit.

3 medium tomatoes, smoked

½ cup yellow onions, chopped

1 Tbsp. garlic, chopped

¼ cup carrots, peeled and chopped

15 oz. can stewed tomatoes

3 cups water

½ cup half and half

3 Tbsp. butter

S ERVES 4 - 6

To best smoke tomatoes, use a stove-top smoker and mesquite or hickory wood chips. Smoke 2–3 minutes or until tomatoes develop a slight bronze color. If you do not have a stove-top smoker, use a pot with a metal colander. Put wood chips in foil and place in the bottom of a pot; place the colander over the pot with tomatoes inside. Cover with foil and poke a couple of pencil-sized holes in the top to let the smoke pass through. Place pot over medium flame, until wood chips begin to smoke.

In a stock pot, over medium heat, sweat onions, garlic and carrots until soft and translucent. Add smoked and stewed tomatoes. Stir and continue cooking 2–3 minutes. Add water and half and half; continue to simmer over medium heat for 4–5 minutes. Place in blender in 3 separate batches, cover tightly and pulse to start. Blend until smooth. Add butter and incorporate.

GRILLED CHEESE DIPPERS

Place cheese slices—cheddar cheese or your favorite—between two slices of sourdough bread. Spray skillet and brown each side over medium-high heat. Cut each into three strips.

SERVING SUGGESTION:
Serve soup with Grilled Cheese Dippers.

CAJUN CORN CHOWDER

THE BACK BOWL SOUP COMPANY • WINTER PARK, COLORADO

The Back Bowl Soup Company is owned and operated by Winter Park locals Steve "Woody" and Jodi Johnson. They deem themselves lucky to be able to combine two of their passions: great food and the amazing Colorado outdoors, complete with powder at their doorstep. All of Back Bowl Soup Company's soups are hand-crafted daily—never served from a bag. Cajun Corn Chowder is a favorite among locals and travelers alike; they hope it becomes a favorite for you, too.

2 Tbsp. butter

2 garlic cloves, chopped

2 large onions, diced

3 cups water

⅓ cup flour

2 cups heavy cream or half and half, divided

2 large potatoes, scrubbed and diced

6 ears Colorado Olatha sweet corn, divided

½ lb. shrimp, raw with shells

1 cup celery, diced

1 red and 1 green bell pepper, diced

2 Tbsp. bacon drippings or olive oil

1 jar clam juice

¼ cup brandy

Cayenne pepper

Gumbo filé powder*

Louisiana hot sauce

SERVES 6

*Gumbo filé powder is a spicy herb made from dried and ground leaves of sassafras trees. It is used to make some types of gumbo, Creole and Cajun soups and stews.

MORE DIFFICULT

Peel shrimp and set aside, reserving shells. Boil shells in water for 20 minutes and strain stock—discard shells and reserve liquid. Cut corn from cobs, reserving both corn and cobs. Toss ¾ of the corn with olive oil and cayenne pepper, spread evenly on a baking sheet and bake at 375 degrees, or until corn starts to tan. Blend remaining corn with 1 cup of heavy cream or half and half until thick and nearly smooth.

Heat butter and bacon drippings in a soup pot over medium heat; add onions, garlic and a few dashes of cayenne pepper. Stir until translucent. Add bell peppers and celery; cook, stirring occasionally, for 5 minutes. Remove from heat and add flour, stirring to coat evenly and gently scraping the pan. Add potatoes and stir; add shrimp stock, clam juice and brandy. Add corn cobs to the pot, and a little water if you need more liquid to cover corn cobs and potatoes. Boil gently until potatoes are soft. Remove corn cobs, add roasted corn and blended creamed corn mixture to the pot. Gently boil, add shrimp meat and remaining cup of cream. Add gumbo filé powder, hot sauce and cayenne pepper to taste.

SERVING SUGGESTION:
Serve soup piping hot with crusty bread and a cold beer.

MANHATTAN CLAM CHOWDER

PLUMPJACK CAFÉ • CHEF BEN "WYATT" DUFRESNE • OLYMPIC VALLEY, CALIFORNIA

The PlumpJack Café's version of Manhattan Clam Chowder adds a little twist by including some ingredients from a Manhattan cocktail (bourbon and bitters). Also, this soup is notoriously dairy-free.

1 cup carrot, medium diced

1 cup celery, medium diced

2 cups yellow onion, medium diced

1 cup green bell pepper, medium diced

⅛ cup garlic, chopped

½ lb. bacon, pasted

1½ lbs. canned diced tomatoes

1 lb. chopped clams, plus juice

1 lb. baby clams

2 oz. Jim Beam bourbon

¾ Tbsp. Tabasco sauce, to taste

⅛ cup Worcestershire sauce, to taste

1 cup russet potatoes, medium diced

½ Tbsp. angostura bitters, to taste

½ Tbsp. kosher salt, to taste

¼ Tbsp. ground black pepper, to taste

5 bay leaves, in sachet

¼ tarragon bunch, in sachet

¼ thyme bunch, in sachet

¼ parsley bunch, in sachet

SERVES 16–20

MOST DIFFICULT

Put bacon in a food processor and puree to a paste. Render bacon in a large rondeau (a wide, round pot that is fairly shallow, allowing steam to disperse quickly for cooking). When mixture is brown, add garlic and cook 5 minutes. Add carrots, celery, onions, and bell peppers; cook until vegetables are tender. Add tomatoes, sachet of herbs and simmer 30 minutes.

Add bourbon and cook 10 minutes. Add clam juice from cans and potatoes; cook about 15 minutes until potatoes are tender. Remove sachet and squeeze-out excess liquid back into the pot. Season with Tabasco, bitters, Worcestershire, salt and pepper. Remove from heat and add clams. Adjust seasoning, if necessary.

SERVING SUGGESTION:
Serve chowder with homemade oyster crackers. Find PlumpJack Cafe's oyster cracker recipe at: SkiTownSoups.com

NORTHWEST STEELHEAD CHOWDER

MT. HOOD BREWING CO. • CHEF JOSHUA BAKER • GOVERNMENT CAMP, OREGON

Located in the middle of three ski areas on Mt. Hood (Mt. Hood Skibowl, Mt. Hood Meadows and Timberline Lodge), Mt. Hood Brewing Co's Northwest Steelhead Chowder was inspired simply by their desire to get the most out of the fresh steelhead filets and their trimmings. This recipe is a delicious twist on the traditional New England Clam Chowder. So, whether you make it in the comfort of your own home or visit the wonderful pub in Government Camp, Oregon, this chowder is guaranteed to warm your tummy on the coldest winter day.

1 oz. butter

1 oz. olive oil

3 large Yukon Gold potatoes, diced

¼ cup garlic, chopped

3 cups yellow onion, diced

3 cups celery, diced

1 cup raw bacon, diced

3 cups clam juice

1 quart heavy cream

1 lb. raw steelhead, diced

Roux

1 Tbsp. Old Bay seasoning

1 Tbsp. thyme

Salt and pepper to taste

SERVES 6–8

 MORE DIFFICULT

In a skillet on medium heat, melt butter and thicken with flour (approximately ½ cup each). Whisk until a thick paste forms. Remove the roux from heat.

In a large pot on medium heat, combine butter and olive oil. Add potatoes, onions, celery, garlic and bacon; cook stirring occasionally until tender. Stir in Old Bay seasoning and thyme, then add clam juice and heavy cream. Heat until warm. Add steelhead and simmer for 10 minutes. Whisk in the roux a little at a time until desired thickness is reached. Season with salt and pepper to taste.

SERVING SUGGESTION:
Garnish soup with oyster crackers and freshly chopped parsley.

BACON BUTTERNUT BISQUE

THE BIG PICTURE THEATER & CAFÉ • CHEF RICHARD SCARZELLO • WAITSFIELD, VERMONT

This famous and beloved Bacon Butternut Bisque was created by Chef Richard Scarzello, whose deep commitment to local ingredients and bacon is perfectly expressed in this special comfort food. Thick and rich with flavors, this soup has become a staple item for the après ski crowd that comes for excellent food and entertainment at "The Big Picture," a movie theater, event space and full-time restaurant. It's a hub of the Mad River community!

¼ cup bacon, diced

1 Tbsp. butter

1 cup white onion, diced

1 garlic clove, chopped

4 cups butternut squash, peeled, seeded and diced

½ cup carrot, peeled and diced

2 cups heavy cream

Water to cover

Salt and pepper to taste, approximately ½ tsp. each

Pure Vermont maple syrup

SERVES 4–6

EASIEST Render bacon. Add butter and melt. Add onions and cook until translucent, stirring frequently. Add garlic and cook for approximately 5 minutes on medium heat. Add butternut squash and carrots; stir. Add heavy cream and water—enough to cover vegetables. Simmer until squash and vegetables are soft, approximately 1 hour.

Puree the soup in a blender and strain through a fine mesh strainer. Season soup with salt, pepper and a hint of maple syrup.

*Amounts are approximated from Chef Scarzello's ingredient list.

To make balsamic reduction: Pour balsamic vinegar into a pan—remember it will reduce by half while cooking. Heat on high and whisk briskly, to prevent burning. Sprinkle with sugar, if desired; vinegar naturally sweetens when reduced. Reduce by half, or until vinegar resembles syrup. Cool.

SERVING SUGGESTION:
Garnish bisque with a drizzle of balsamic reduction.

NOOKSACK RIVER'S CLAM CHOWDER

CANOE RIVER RESTAURANT • CHEF BRANDON YATES • DEMING, WASHINGTON

For 5 years, Nooksack River's Clam Chowder has been a staple recipe, with only minor changes to herbs and amounts. But, "the core has remained the same," states Executive Chef Brandon Yates. Chef Yates has been delighting palettes in Pacific Northwest restaurants for years.

¼ lb. bacon, diced

¾ cup butter

¼ lb. celery, diced

¼ lb. onion, diced

¼ cup garlic, minced

¾ cup flour

3 lbs. clams, chopped

6 cups clam juice

4 cups heavy cream

2 cups half and half

4 cups 2% milk

Tabasco sauce to taste

1 bay leaf

4 tsp. dried thyme

3 tsp. black pepper, freshly ground

¼ lb. clam base

12 red potatoes, approximately ¼-inch diced

SERVES 10–12

MORE DIFFICULT

Sauté the bacon until fat is rendered and bacon starts to crisp, incorporate the butter. As butter melts, add onions, garlic and celery. Mix in flour. Once flour is incorporated, add milk and whisk until smooth. Add clams, clam juice, heavy cream, half and half, spices and herbs. Bring all ingredients to a gentle simmer. Add clam base, if needed for taste.

Finally, include the red potatoes and cook for an hour, or until potatoes start to soften.

SERVING SUGGESTION:

This clam chowder is best accompanied by a warm baguette or oyster crackers. You may also try serving it in a bread bowl.

ARTICHOKE & BLUE CHEESE BISQUE

TAMARACK BREWING COMPANY • LAKESIDE, MONTANA

Tamarack Brewing Company lives its motto, "Think Local, Drink Local," and this Artichoke and Blue Cheese Bisque is a perfect recipe for them to share! Tamarack Brewing Company is nestled beneath the Rocky and Mission Mountains in Lakeside, Montana, near the shores of beautiful Flathead Lake. High ceilings, fascinating architectural details and a warm ambience help make "The 'Rack", as known to locals, the best spot in the Flathead Valley to relax with great food and hand-crafted ales.

4 Tbsp. butter

1 large white onion, diced

⅓ cup Tamarack Brewing Company Bear Bottom Blonde Ale, or other light ale

24 oz. artichoke hearts, drained

8 cups chicken stock

2 Tbsp. dried thyme

2 cups heavy cream

½ cup blue cheese, crumbled

Salt and pepper to taste

Chives, chopped

SERVES 10

In a large pot, sauté onion in butter until translucent. Add beer and bring to a simmer. Add artichoke hearts, chicken stock and thyme. Simmer until artichokes fall apart. Let mixture cool and puree in a blender or with an immersion blender. Strain through a sieve, and return to the pot.

Add cream and return to a low simmer. Add cheese slowly and whisk until cheese is melted and soup is smooth. Season with salt and pepper.

SERVING SUGGESTION:
Garnish with chives before serving.

SEAFOOD CHOWDER

HEARTH & CANDLE • JEFFERSONVILLE, VERMONT

The Hearth & Candle is a privately-operated restaurant in the heart of Smugglers' Notch Resort, where the chefs specialize in fresh, local ingredients for everyone's enjoyment!

2 celery stalks, diced

½ onion, diced

1½ cups russet potato, diced

1 garlic clove, minced

½ cup white wine

8 oz. can clam juice

½ lb. clams, chopped

1 Tbsp. clam base

½ tsp. ground rosemary

½ tsp. oregano

½ tsp. black pepper

½ tsp. thyme

¼ cup flour

¼ cup butter

¼ lb. scallops, chopped

½ lb. baby shrimp

Heavy cream

SERVES 4–6

MORE DIFFICULT

In a stock pot, sauté celery, onions and garlic until translucent, then add white wine. Pour in clam juice, potatoes and clams, add clam base and herbs; bring to a boil.

In a separate skillet, make a roux: combine flour and butter; stir until completely mixed. Cook for 5 minutes.

Whisk small amounts of roux into stock pot. Cook for several minutes, then add shrimp and scallops. Stir until scallops are cooked. Remove from heat.

Whisk in cream until desired consistency is achieved.

SERVING SUGGESTION:
This decadent Seafood Chowder does not need any embellishments, before serving, but you may add a sprig of rosemary for visual appeal.

APPLE BUTTERNUT BISQUE

FABYANS STATION • CHEF NICHOLAS RENEY • BRETTON WOODS, NEW HAMPSHIRE

When most visitors traveled by train, this was the stop for those venturing into New Hampshire's magnificent Crawford Notch. As one of the original railroad stations, restored and converted to a restaurant and lounge, Fabyans Station is located across from Bretton Woods Mountain Resort and the alpine skiing area.

10 butternut squash, peeled and chopped

20 golden delicious apples, peeled, seeded and halved

5 white onions, chopped

15 garlic cloves, crushed

8 carrots, peeled and chopped

6 cinnamon sticks

3 quarts apple juice

2 quarts heavy cream

2 cups brown sugar

1 cup honey

1 Tbsp. ground nutmeg

SERVES 12–14

Sauté onions, garlic and carrots. Add remaining ingredients and bring to a simmer. Slowly cook until all vegetables are tender. Remove all cinnamon sticks. Puree in a blender or with an immersion blender. Salt and pepper to taste.

SERVING SUGGESTION:
This fragrant soup will awaken your senses without needing any garnishes.

LOBSTER BISQUE

HEARTHSTONE RESTAURANT • CHEF MICHAEL HALPIN • BRECKENRIDGE, COLORADO

Hearthstone Restaurant, recognized by local readers of the Summit Daily News as the "Best Restaurant in Summit County", serves this bisque with genuine Colorado hospitality! This may be the perfect soup for special occasions, such as New Year's Eve and Christmas. Hearthstone Restaurant, located in the heart of the Rocky Mountains in Breckenridge, Colorado, is housed in the historic, 125 year-old Kaiser House, a richly decorated Victorian-era home. From here, you will enjoy the beautiful views across town to the slopes of the Breckenridge Ski Resort and the Ten Mile Range.

4 lbs. lobster shells

1 cup tomato paste

¾ cup brandy

¾ cup sherry

1 large yellow onion, chopped

1 fennel bulb, chopped

⅜ cup fresh tarragon, chopped

½ celery bunch, chopped

3 quarts fish stock

2 cups heavy cream

4 lobster claws

⅜ cup butter

⅜ cup flour

⅜ cup soybean oil

SERVES 6–8

MOST DIFFICULT

In a large pot on medium-high heat, sauté lobster shells in soybean oil until completely red. Do not burn. Add onions, fennel and celery. Add tomato paste and stir. Deglaze with brandy and sherry. Add fish stock and tarragon. Heat until reduced by half.

While this is reducing, melt butter in a small saucepan and add flour to make a roux, then set aside. When soup has reduced by half, strain into a new pot, bring to a boil and add cream. Reduce heat and simmer; whisk in the roux. Cook on low heat for approximately 30 minutes.

Lightly sauté the lobster claw meat in butter for use as a garnish.

SERVING SUGGESTION:
In the center of a bowl, place lobster claw meat on a puff pastry box or crostini and sprinkle with fresh tarragon. Pour soup around this.

CHICKEN CORN CHOWDER

THE BASEBOX LODGE • CHEF MICHAEL WITZEL • WAITSFIELD, VERMONT

In 1995, a new era began when the Mad River Glen Cooperative was formed—the first cooperatively owned ski area in America. Mad River Glen remains independent, preserving a ski experience that exists nowhere else. Shareholders in the Mad River Glen Cooperative have come together to fulfill their mission; ". . . to preserve and protect the forests and mountain ecosystem of General Stark Mountain in order to provide skiing and other recreational access and to maintain the unique character of the area for present and future generations."

½ lb. bacon, medium diced

1 onion, medium diced

½ Tbsp. garlic, chopped

½ chipotle pepper, minced
(canned with a little sauce)

4 oz. butter

1½ cups flour

8 oz. apple cider

32 oz. chicken stock

½ celery bunch, medium diced

½ lb. chicken, cooked and diced

1½ lbs. Yukon gold potatoes, diced

3–16 oz. cans sweet corn

½ Tbsp. dried parsley

½ Tbsp. dried rosemary

10–16 oz. heavy cream,
half and half or milk

Salt and pepper to taste

Tabasco sauce to taste (optional)

SERVES 10–12

EASIEST

In a heavy-bottomed stock pot, render bacon until crispy. Do not drain. Add onions, garlic, chipotle peppers and butter; cook until tender. Add flour and stir, making a roux. Cook until incorporated. Deglaze with apple cider, stirring until smooth. Add remaining ingredients, including liquid from corn. Simmer until potatoes are tender, about 1 hour.

Add choice of dairy. Adjust seasoning with salt, black pepper and Tabasco.

SERVING SUGGESTION:
As natural as the Mad River Glen Cooperative mission statement, serve this soup unadorned.

ROASTED TOMATO BISQUE

HARLEY & BUCK'S • CHEF CRAIG BONHAM • EDEN, UTAH

There is nothing better, after a day on the ski slopes or in the middle of a snowstorm, than comfort food! Craig Bonham, Owner and Chef of Harley & Buck's in Eden, Utah, loves to take traditional recipes and give them a new twist. Lobster Mac and Cheese and Roasted Tomato Bisque are two of his favorite comfort foods . . . with a twist!

2 Tbsp. olive oil

1 cup onion, ¼-inch diced

5–6 large tomatoes (approximately 3 lbs.)

2 cups tomato stock (2 cups of water mixed with 1½ Tbsp. Caldo de Tomate or Chicken Base)

2 Tbsp. balsamic vinegar

½ Tbsp. dried thyme

1 cup heavy cream

½ cup parmesan, shredded

¼ cup fresh basil, coarsely chopped

SERVES 4

 EASIEST

Wash tomatoes and cut into 1-inch thick slices. Place tomatoes on an oiled sheet and cook in a 375 degree oven for 20 minutes.

While tomatoes are cooking, heat olive oil in a large stock pot. Add onions and cook on medium heat for 6–8 minutes until onions are translucent. Add cooked tomatoes, thyme and tomato stock. Bring to a boil. Reduce heat and simmer uncovered for 20 minutes.

Add balsamic vinegar and heavy cream. Puree with an immersion blender until smooth.

SERVING SUGGESTION:

Sprinkle bisque with shredded parmesan cheese and fresh basil. Pair with a grilled cheese sandwich, garlic croutons, or Chef Craig's previously mentioned Lobster Mac and Cheese. (This recipe is available at SkiTownSoups.com.)

BUTTERNUT SQUASH BISQUE
with Pomegranate Salsa

FLORADORA SALOON • TELLURIDE, COLORADO

Conveniently located on Main Street in the heart of historic downtown Telluride, Colorado, the Floradora Saloon is a Western-style saloon with a menu featuring fresh, crisp flavors using natural and organic ingredients from the region.

3 lbs. butternut squash, peeled and seeded

2 yellow onions, chopped

1 Tbsp. garlic, minced

2 tsp. ginger, minced

3 bay leaves

3 Tbsp. white wine

4 quarts lemongrass stock, (See recipe)

Salt and pepper to taste

SERVES 6–8

MOST DIFFICULT

Place butternut squash on an oiled sheet and roast in a 375 oven for 1 hour and 20 minutes, or until tender. Sweat onions in a large pot on medium heat with a small amount of oil until onions are translucent. Add garlic and ginger; cook for 1 minute. Add white wine to deglaze. Remove and discard peels from squash. Add stock, squash and bay leaves to other ingredients; simmer for 1 hour. Remove bay leaves.

In a blender, or with an immersion blender, puree the soup. Adjust seasoning to taste.

LEMONGRASS STOCK

1 onion, chopped

3 carrots, chopped

1 celery bunch, chopped

¼ lb. lemongrass, chopped

1 tsp. black peppercorns

2 garlic cloves, minced

3 tsp. thyme

2 bay leaves

4 quarts water

1 quart ice

6 tsp. ginger

Combine all ingredients in a large stock pot. Lightly simmer for 1 hour, do not boil. Strain through a China cap. Reserve liquid and discard solids.

POMEGRANATE SALSA

1 red bell pepper, diced

1 green bell pepper, diced

1 red onion, diced

1 oz. ginger, candied and diced

1 jalapeño pepper, diced

2 pomegranates

2 Tbsp. cilantro, chopped

1 lime, juiced

Salt and pepper to taste

Place peppers, onions, jalapeño and ginger in mixing bowl. Quarter the pomegranates, remove all the seeds and add seeds to salsa mixture. Add cilantro. Halve the lime and squeeze the juice over ingredients. Salt and pepper to taste.

SERVING SUGGESTION:
Serve bisque with a dollop of Pomegranate Salsa.

NEW ENGLAND CLAM CHOWDER

CHIMNEY ROCK GRILL • CHEF KELLEY KENNEDY • SANDPOINT, IDAHO

Chimney Rock Grill and Schweitzer Mountain Resort are located in the land-locked panhandle of northern Idaho. But, Chef Kelley Kennedy and the Food and Beverage Director at Schweitzer Mountain are both from New England, so the name of the soup is not quite as off-base as one might imagine. What started out as simple soup-making turned into a craze—as Idaho potatoes compliment this New England Clam Chowder very well. This chowder has been available at the restaurant for 10 years' worth of ski seasons and will not be leaving. In this soup, East meets West and are living (and eating) blissfully together!

5 slices bacon, thick-cut and diced

1 large white onion, diced

4 celery stalks, diced

½ cup butter

10 cups clam juice (canned clam juice or any seafood stock)

1½ cups flour

3½ cups clams, chopped

5 Idaho red potatoes

1 bay leaf

1½ tsp. Old Bay seasoning

1 tsp. thyme

1 Tbsp. lemon juice, juice from ½ lemon

3 cups half and half

1 Tbsp. Tabasco sauce

Salt and pepper to taste

SERVES 6–8

MOST DIFFICULT

Cut red potatoes into bite-size cubes, cover with cold water in a medium size pot and boil until soft. Do not over boil. Set potatoes aside.

In a heavy-bottomed pot over medium heat, brown bacon until crispy. Add onion and celery and cook with crispy bacon bits until vegetables are slightly translucent. Add butter to the pot and melt completely. Slowly add flour in 3 batches, stirring constantly, until all butter is absorbed by flour. Stir and cook flour for approximately 2 minutes, until just brown.

Add clam juice and stir until flour incorporates with the juice. Scrape the bottom of the pot as you stir. Add clams, cooked potatoes, bay leaf, Old Bay seasoning, thyme, lemon juice, half and half, Tabasco, salt and pepper. Continue to cook on medium heat until soup is hot. Do not boil. Continue stirring so nothing settles and burns.

SERVING SUGGESTION:

Oyster crackers are a "must have" if you want the true New England experience!

CREAMY MUSHROOM BISQUE

ORANGE CAT CAFÉ • KINGFIELD, MAINE

This soup, even though it's simple and easy, is one of the most popular soups offered at Orange Cat Café! The homemade vegetable stock has an indescribable earthy flavor. The café believes in using high-quality ingredients, including local and organic produce, when available. One trick Orange Cat Café uses for all their creamy soups is substituting cream cheese for the base, instead of heavy cream. This provides a creamy texture without the heaviness from the cream.

1½ sticks salted butter

2 lbs. crimini mushrooms (baby-bella), sliced

6 large portabella mushrooms, sliced

1 lb. button mushrooms, sliced

1 large red onion, chopped

5 garlic cloves, minced

1 large red bell pepper, chopped

4 celery stalks, chopped

1 tsp. salt

1 tsp. black pepper

Fresh parsley

1½ tsp. nutmeg, freshly grated

½ tsp. dry mustard

½ tsp. red pepper flakes (optional)

16 oz. softened cream cheese

2½ cups shaved parmesan and asiago cheeses

1 gallon homemade vegetable stock

EASIEST

Sauté in butter, red onions, celery, bell peppers, garlic, salt, pepper, nutmeg, dried mustard and red pepper flakes in a large soup pot over medium heat. While vegetables are softening, add sliced mushrooms. Add more butter, if needed. Cook until everything is nicely browned and soft. Remove and reserve ¼ of the sautéed vegetables in a separate container.

Add homemade vegetable stock and simmer for 30–45 minutes. In a food processor, blend soup with cream cheese in several batches. Return soup to pot. Add shredded cheeses and reserved vegetables and heat until cheese melts. Add more vegetable stock if soup is too thick. Add salt and pepper to taste.

SERVING SUGGESTION:
Serve soup topped with fresh parsley and accompany with homemade honey-oat bread.

ROASTED TOMATO BISQUE

JJ'S ROCKY MOUNTAIN TAVERN • CHEF JUSTIN PETERSON • COPPER MOUNTAIN, COLORADO

Titanic survivor, Molly Brown (née Margaret Tobin), moved to Leadville, Colorado, where she met and married miner James Joseph ("JJ") Brown—namesake for JJ's Rocky Mountain Tavern. Featured on the restaurant's menu is "The Maggie". This signature lunch special features pit-smoked ham, Fontina cheese, Dijon mayo on thick sliced sourdough bread, a Caesar salad and a cup of the famous Roasted Tomato Bisque. JJ's Rocky Mountain Tavern boasts the longest bar in Summit County and is decorated to reflect taverns during the late 1800s and early 1900s. There are many Titanic references and pictures of JJ and Molly Brown throughout the restaurant.

5 lbs. Roma tomatoes

1½ cups fresh shallots

½ cup whole garlic bulbs

¼ cup olive oil

1 cup red wine

1 quart diced tomatoes in juice

1 quart tomato juice

2 Tbsp. parmesan rind

2 cups heavy cream

1 cup fresh basil

Salt and pepper to taste

SERVES 4–6

 EASIEST

Preheat oven to 425 degrees. Slice or core out ends of Roma tomatoes and place on roasting pan. Cut shallots in half and smash whole garlic bulbs; combine these with tomatoes. Add olive oil to tomatoes, onions and garlic; toss well. Roast for 15–20 minutes until nicely browned, almost charred.

Remove from oven and pour tomato mixture into heavy-bottomed stock pot on stove. Add wine to the roasting pan and scrape any roasted bits into pot with the wine. Add diced tomatoes and tomato juice to pot and simmer for 15 minutes.

Puree tomato mixture with an immersion blender or in batches in a food processor. Return to pot. Add heavy cream, fresh basil, parmesan rind, salt and pepper. Simmer for 25 minutes and remove parmesan rind. Adjust seasoning.

SERVING SUGGESTION:
Garnish with a fresh sprig of basil, cheddar croutons, or mini grilled cheese sandwiches.

SKI VERMONT FARMHOUSE POTATO CHOWDER

SUGARBUSH RESORT • CHEF GERRY NOONEY • WARREN, VERMONT

Gerry Nooney, Sugarbush Resort's Executive Chef and Food and Beverage Director, recently won Vermont's Chef of the Year. This accolade can be credited to the combination of this recipe and his commitment to sourcing local ingredients for all his cooking. Chef Nooney was asked to assist Vermont's potato farmers in increasing sales. Happy to help, he created Ski Vermont Farmhouse Potato Chowder, which is now offered at all of the Vermont ski areas, some schools, and other venues— reinforcing the importance of having a regional food supply.

1 quart chicken stock

¾ cup Vermont cider

12 oz. Vermont potatoes, peeled and chopped

2 Tbsp. vegetable oil

1 small Spanish onion, small diced

2 celery stalks, small diced

1 tsp. smoked paprika

1 link hot Italian sausage

1 tsp. whole leaf dried marjoram

1 tsp. whole leaf dried basil

1 tsp. kosher salt

Freshly ground black pepper to taste

½ cup heavy cream

½ lb. Vermont potatoes, large diced

SERVES 4–6

MORE DIFFICULT

Simmer 12 oz. of potatoes in chicken stock and cider until very tender. Puree in blender and return to a large stock pot.

Roast hot Italian sausage until cooked through. Chill sausage and pulse in food processor—not too fine. Add sausage to pureed soup mixture.

In a separate pan, sweat onions and celery in vegetable oil until translucent. Add smoked paprika and cook for 3 minutes, stirring often. Add this mixture to pureed soup/sausage mixture. Stir in cream.

In a medium pot, simmer large diced potatoes in salted water until tender. Drain and rinse under cold water. Add potatoes to soup mixture. Add marjoram, basil, salt and pepper to soup. Simmer the soup.

SERVING SUGGESTION:
Without any garnishing, the chowder stands very well on its own.

AWARD-WINNING CHART HOUSE
CLAM CHOWDER

CHART HOUSE • MAMMOTH LAKES, CALIFORNIA

Chart House's phenomenal Clam Chowder has built quite the reputation! Having won the Boston Chowderfest 3 times (1989, 1990 and 1995), Chart House is no longer allowed to compete in the famous event. However, Chart House still attends the competition annually, as a member of the illustrious Chowderfest Hall of Fame, to showcase their award-winning chowder. This chowder is creamy, not too salty and has a great mixture of potatoes and clams—people are constantly singing its praises!

4 oz. salted butter

3½ oz. flour

¼ cup clam broth

25 oz. ocean clams, chopped with juice

8 oz. celery, ¼-inch diced

2 cups red potatoes, ¼-inch diced

2 cups half and half

¼ tsp. dried thyme

1 tsp. Worcestershire sauce

¼ tsp. Tabasco sauce

2 tsp. black pepper

SERVES 4–6

MORE DIFFICULT

In a sauté pan, melt butter over medium heat. Slowly whisk in flour to make a roux. When fully combined, remove mixture from heat and set aside.

In a stock pot, add remaining ingredients and stir together over high heat. Boil and reduce heat to a simmer for approximately 25 minutes. Once potatoes are tender, add roux mixture. Let soup simmer for an additional 10 minutes. Season to taste.

SERVING SUGGESTION:
This soup is best served fresh in a crusty, sourdough bread bowl.

IRISH CHICKEN CHOWDER

ROOSEVELT GRILLE • KETCHUM, IDAHO

This recipe was given to Roosevelt Grille by one of their chefs who worked in a pub in Ireland for many years. Irish Chicken Chowder is a hearty, wholesome chowder. After a day on the slopes of the Sun Valley Resort, head to Ketchum (adjacent to Sun Valley) where you can enjoy this soup at Roosevelt Grille, a classic ski-town restaurant.

4 oz. carrots, diced

4 oz. yellow onion, diced

4 oz. celery, diced

4 oz. butter

½ cup flour

½ gallon chicken stock

8 oz. chicken breast, cooked and diced

¾ lb. potatoes, diced

½ quart half and half

¾ cup green peas

1 tsp. salt

1 tsp. ground black pepper

SERVES 4–6

EASIEST

Melt butter and sauté the vegetables until soft. Add flour and stir to form a roux. Remove the roux and vegetables from the pot and set aside.

Add chicken stock to pot and bring to a simmer. Add diced potatoes and cook for 10 minutes. Add cooked chicken and return to a simmer. Mix in roux/vegetable mixture, salt, pepper and half and half. Return to simmer until soup thickens. Turn off heat and add green peas.

SERVING SUGGESTION:
Best served with crusty sourdough bread and a medium-bodied Pilsner.

SOUTHWESTERN CHICKEN CHOWDER

ENDO'S ADRENALINE CAFÉ • CHEF PHIL BRADY • COPPER MOUNTAIN, COLORADO

Southwestern Chicken Chowder is a tried-and-true menu item featured at Endo's Adrenaline Café since 2001. This chowder is prepared from scratch daily with all-natural, locally-sourced chicken breasts, fresh vegetables, freshly prepared chicken stock and sweet cream. Thick, hearty and containing a good kick of heat and spices, Endo's signature Southwestern Chicken Chowder is a crowd favorite year after year.

3 Tbsp. garlic, minced

1 cup onion, diced

½ cup celery, diced

1 red pepper, diced

3 quarts chicken stock

½ cup roux

2 Tbsp. dark chili powder

2 tsp. cumin

2 tsp. oregano

2 Tbsp. salt

1 Tbsp. pepper

1 lb. chicken, cooked and diced

1 lb. potatoes, diced

3½ cups heavy cream

2 cups corn

¼ cup bacon, chopped

½ cup cilantro, chopped

SERVES 6–8

 EASIEST

In a skillet on medium heat, melt butter and thicken with flour (approximately ¼–½ cup each). Whisk until a roux is made and a paste forms. Remove from heat.

In a stock pot, sauté garlic, bacon, onion and celery until caramelized. Add red peppers, chicken stock, dark chili powder, cumin, oregano, potatoes, salt and pepper. Simmer until potatoes are soft. Stir in roux until desired thickness is reached. Add heavy cream, corn, cilantro and chicken. Heat to a hot serving temperature.

SERVING SUGGESTION:
No embellishments are needed for this rich, filling chowder.

CHURCH'S CHOWDER

FOUR-TIME "SOUPSKÖL" WINNER • CHEF CLARK CHURCH • SNOWMASS, COLORADO

Chef Clark Church, former Chef and Owner of Garnish Restaurant & Catering in Aspen/Snowmass, is famous in the area for his soups! Garnish Restaurant & Catering was established in 2007, though now Chef Church has relocated to Parker, Colorado, as Executive Chef at The Pinery Country Club. Church's Chowder, not only a 3-peat champion of Aspen's Soupsköl, was recognized in Summer 2009 Aspen Magazine's Bucket List as one of the 87 Feel Good Things to Eat Before You Die.

½ lb. unsalted butter

½ lb. all-purpose flour

1 yellow onion, diced

5 celery stalks, diced

5 garlic cloves, minced

4 Idaho or russet potatoes, peeled and diced
(kept in water to prevent from browning)

½ gallon whole milk

1 lb. clams, fresh-shucked
(or 2–8 oz. canned clams in juice)

12 oz. clam juice, if using fresh clams

⅛ cup Old Bay seasoning

⅛ cup lemon pepper

¼ cup fresh chives, chiffonade
(cut into long, thin strips)

¼ cup Italian parsley, chopped

Salt and pepper to taste

SERVES 6–8

In a medium soup pot on medium heat, add butter and melt. Add garlic, onions and celery; cook approximately 10 minutes. Add shucked clams and cook for 5 minutes. Add flour to make the roux and cook for several minutes to incorporate flour. (If using canned clams, add flour first to make roux and then add clams). Add milk and clam juice, then cook until base thickens; stir often to prevent burning. To achieve desired consistency, soup must boil.

In a separate pot, bring salted water to a rolling boil. Strain water from diced potatoes; add potatoes to boiling water. Cook until almost tender, strain, and add potatoes to soup base.

Add lemon pepper and Old Bay seasoning. Simmer on low heat for at least an hour; stir often to prevent burning. Add chives and parsley; cook another 10–15 minutes. Adjust seasoning with salt and pepper.

SERVING SUGGESTION:
Serve with oyster crackers.

CHESAPEAKE BAY CRAB CHOWDER

SUMMIT SALOON • BEND, OREGON

In 2007, the Summit opened its doors in the historic O'Kane Building located in downtown Bend, Oregon. In 2010, Sunset Magazine named Bend as the 'Best Ski Town for Foodies' with its variety of fine dining and more casual restaurants both downtown and in the Old Mill District.

1 quart carrots, finely chopped

1 quart celery, finely chopped

1 quart onion, finely chopped

1 lb. blue crab claw and body meat

1 gallon chicken and/or vegetable stock

5 cups Yukon potatoes, diced

¾ gallon heavy cream

1 cup white wine

3 cups flour

¾ lb. butter

¼ cup salt

⅛ cup pepper

⅓ cup Old Bay seasoning

½ tsp. tarragon

½ tsp. thyme

SERVES 10–12

MORE DIFFICULT

Sauté carrots, celery, and onions in butter until the vegetables are tender and onions are translucent. Add flour and stir continuously, about 5 minutes. Deglaze with wine. Add stock. Stir in potatoes and crab meat. Simmer until potatoes soften, about 20 minutes.

Add heavy cream and heat—do not boil. Add salt, pepper, herbs and spices. Stir and adjust seasoning to taste.

SERVING SUGGESTION:

For visual appeal, garnish with a sprig of thyme. To get a smile from guests, pronounce this soup "chowdah".

SHRIMP & LOBSTER BISQUE

GAR WOODS GRILL & PIER • CHEF ROBERT PHILLIPS • CARNELIAN BAY, CALIFORNIA

Gar Woods Grill, a comfortable dining environment that captures the nostalgic ambiance of Tahoe's classic wooden boat era, is located in the original location of the historic Carnelian Bay Hotel. It seems only fitting that the restaurant that bears the name "Gar Woods" be found on Lake Tahoe, close to the Sierra Boat Company, as Garfield (Gar) Woods was an historical figure in the sport of boating.

2 cups white wine

3 Tbsp. shallots, diced

1 tsp. garlic, chopped

½ cup lobster base

5 cups milk

7 cups heavy cream

8 Tbsp. butter

8 Tbsp. flour

1 tsp. paprika

1 tsp. Tabasco

Chives

Rock shrimp

½ cup sherry

SERVES 6–8

MORE DIFFICULT

In a small pan, melt butter and mix in flour. Whisk and cook for a couple of minutes to make a roux, then cool.

In a large soup pot, combine shallots and white wine; reduce by half. Add garlic and cook for 2 minutes. Add lobster base and sherry and mix until smooth. Add milk and cream; simmer. Add Tabasco and paprika to the soup. Then, slowly whisk in the roux, do not scrape the bottom. Simmer soup for at least 8 minutes. Strain through a china cap (fine mesh strainer).

FLEURONS (SOUP PUFFS)

¼ sheet puff pastry

6 egg yolks, beaten

Cut puff pastry into half moons, approximately 16, and place on a sheet pan. Paint with egg wash and bake at 350 degrees for 20 minutes.

SERVING SUGGESTION:
Place a rock shrimp in a soup bowl, over which ladle hot bisque. Garnish with diced chives and 2 Fleurons.

SEAFOOD CHOWDER

158 MAIN • CHEF JOHN FOLEY • JEFFERSONVILLE, VERMONT

158 Main is housed in the historic Windridge Farms building, nestled in the village of Jeffersonville, Vermont—just a one minute drive to skiing at the Smugglers' Notch Resort. Chef John Foley has made a study of Vermont and the reality of what, when, where and how local foods are available to Vermont chefs. That's what inspired Chef Foley to create Seafood Chowder, which helped put 158 Main on the culinary map of Vermont.

1 cup carrots, diced

1 cup celery, diced

1 cup onions, diced

2 cups potatoes, diced

1 quart lobster stock

1 quart heavy cream

1 lb. (31–40) shrimp, peeled and cleaned

1 lb. clams, shucked

1 lb. haddock, diced

Thyme sprig

SERVES 6–8

MOST DIFFICULT

In a large pot, sauté all vegetables for 10 minutes. Add lobster stock and heavy cream; simmer for 15 minutes. Add all seafood and simmer another 15 minutes.

LOBSTER STOCK

4 lbs. lobster bodies

2 carrots, diced

2 celery stalks, diced

1 onion, diced

1 Tbsp. tomato paste

Olive oil

3 quarts cold water

In a pot, sauté lobster bodies, tomato paste and vegetables, with a bit of olive oil, for 20 minutes or until vegetables are soft. Add water and bring to a boil. Reduce heat and simmer for 1 hour. Strain stock and reserve.

SERVING SUGGESTION:
Garnish chowder with a sprig of thyme.

STONE HARBOR CRAB BISQUE

FORTY-ONE SOUTH • SAGLE, IDAHO

Forty-One South offers beautiful, waterfront fine dining overlooking Lake Pend Oreille with breathtaking sunset views in a romantic lodge setting. Forty-One South strives to use local ingredients, as well as herbs and vegetables from their own garden. Stone Harbor Crab Bisque is one of their most popular menu items and is served year 'round.

1 cup all-purpose flour

1 cup canola oil

8 cups milk

8 cups heavy whipping cream

3½ Tbsp. crab base

¾ cup dry sherry

1 lb. Dungeness, Lump Red or Blue Swimming Crab

Chives, minced

SERVES 6 – 8

EASIEST

In a large stainless steel pot on medium high, add oil and flour to make a roux. Whisk rapidly to remove all lumps. Do not let roux brown. Add milk in 4-cup increments; thoroughly heat before adding the next (first increment should form a smooth paste).

Once milk is added and hot, add cream, base and sherry. Increase heat to high and bring soup to a boil, stirring frequently. Reduce to a simmer for 15 minutes, stirring occasionally. Strain though a fine mesh strainer. Gently stir in crab.

SERVING SUGGESTION:
Garnish soup with minced chives.

Aspen's Annual Soupsköl

Aspen's Annual Wintersköl Celebration has a festive soup-cooking contest judged by the public to determine which restaurant has the best soup in town. It's called Soupsköl! The competition gives the winner bragging rights for the entire next year! Over 3,000 locals and tourists attend the event and every year it grows in popularity. It is designed to bring friendly competition to the restaurants within the Roaring Fork Valley.

Chef Clark Church and his team won the Soupsköl competition for 4 years straight (2007–2009 for Church's Chowder and 2010 for Wisconsin Beer Cheese Soup). Church's Chowder, a New England Clam Chowder, is hearty and hot and served with a smile. Merry-Go-Round, the 2011 Soupsköl winner, is also highlighted in this cookbook! Ute City, the 2012 champion, is also showcased with their winning soup recipe—Red Bell Pepper Parmesan Soup.

See page 96 for Chef Clark Church's Chowder.

See page 47 for Chef Rob MacClanahan's Red Bell Pepper Parmesan Soup.

See page 137 for Chef de Cuisine Phil House's Beef and Barley Stew.

Sowing Seeds

Ski Town Soups has partnered with the Sowing Seeds program—a project of the Vail Valley Foundation's Youth Foundation. The foundation identifies gaps and develops, evaluates and funds programs to fulfill youth's needs. One of these programs is Sowing Seeds (est. 2010), wherein a portion of profits from the *Ski Town Soups* cookbook will be allocated. Sowing Seeds works with schools to integrate gardening into their curriculum, thus incorporating fresh produce into the school cafeteria offerings. Ultimately, this connects children to the environment, fosters understanding of the origin of food, and teaches responsibility through stimulating hands-on activities, such as planting gardens.

Recently, Sowing Seeds received a major success; they were awarded a grant from the Lowe's Toolbox for Education program. In a Vail Daily article, Susie Davis, the vice president of education for the VVF's Youth Foundation, stated, "This community-minded, 'farm-to-table' mentality is invaluable in teaching the students the value of working together to make healthy impacts on each other's lives."

James Walt

Executive Chef James Walt of Araxi Restaurant + Bar in Whistler, British Columbia, Canada, continues to inspire both his contemporaries and his guests, creating compelling regional cuisine based on local, sustainable ingredients. His impressive culinary career spans some of British Columbia's leading restaurants, as well as an appointment as Executive Chef to The Canadian Embassy in Rome, an experience that has shaped the way he cooks today. "The European market culture has inspired me to cook even more locally and seasonally," he says. "There, if it's not local and in season, it's simply not served. Everything is sold at its prime so you're able to shop daily—ideal circumstances for being creative and spontaneous."

Chef Walt is now a champion of local products and has developed strong relationships with local farmers in the nearby Pemberton Valley, where the rich, alluvial soil yields some of British Columbia's finest produce. Those crops of fruits and vegetables find themselves onto Chef James Walt's and Araxi's menus every day. In addition, local ranchers and coastal fishermen are well featured at Araxi—Pemberton beef and other local game meats are very popular items, while Araxi's well-known Raw Bar boasts many varieties of oysters, prawns, scallops and fin fish, delivered fresh daily. Additionally, Chef James is Whistler's only chef to have cooked at the celebrated James Beard House in New York City—an unprecedented three times!

After 30 years, Araxi remains a success with Chef James Walt at the helm! Chef Gordon Ramsay rates it as the best in Canada, and the restaurant was widely featured on his FOX-TV program "Hell's Kitchen"—the prize for the winning chef of Hell's Kitchen was an apprenticeship at Araxi and the ability to work with renowned chef, James Walt.

See page 173 for Chef James Walt's Dungeness Crab and Coconut Milk Soup.

Traci Des Jardins

Traci Des Jardins is Chef and Co-owner of Jardinière and Mijita Cocina Mexicana. She is also Chef and Partner of Public House and Manzanita. She is the quintessential California farm girl, raised in the San Joaquin Valley, influenced by her Mexican and French Acadian grandparents. Above all else, she cooks from her heart with a deep love for the earth and its bounty!

James Beard award-winning chef, Traci Des Jardins, continues to earn a great number of accolades, including the James Beard Foundation's "Rising Star Chef of the Year" in 1995 while at Rubicon; Food & Wine Magazine's "Best New Chef"; San Francisco Magazine's "Chef of the Year"; and the James Beard Foundation Award in 2007 for "Best Chef: Pacific". Additionally, in 1999, Jardinière won Esquire Magazine's "Best New Restaurant" as well as a nomination by the James Beard foundation for "Best New Restaurant". The San Francisco Chronicle has listed Jardinière as one of the "Top 100 Restaurants" in the Bay Area each year since opening. In 2007, Traci beat Iron Chef Mario Batali on the Food Network show Iron Chef America; she also competed on Bravo's Top Chef Masters 3, where she made it to the final three contestants.

In 2009, combining her love of California and skiing, Traci opened Manzanita, her destination mountain restaurant in the new Ritz-Carlton at Northstar in Lake Tahoe. Taking its name from the ubiquitous California tree, Manzanita offers Traci's signature French inspired California cuisine, with a regional mountain resort influence, sourcing organic, sustainable and locally grown meat and produce.

Traci is a deeply committed activist and philanthropist working with hunger relief organizations such as Share Our Strength, Citymeals On-Wheels and with other non-profits such as La Cocina and amfAR.

See page 2 for Chef Traci Des Jardins' Kabocha Squash Soup.

STEWS
& CHILIES

FRESHIES VEGETARIAN TOFU CHILI

FRESHIES • CHEF ERIK ULMAN • SOUTH LAKE TAHOE, CALIFORNIA

Don't be afraid of tofu, states Chef Erik Ulman! When he first met Melodie, his wife and restaurant partner, she was a long-time vegetarian—a touch intimidating—but as a chef, he was up to the challenge. He now believes vegetarian food can be as, if not more, flavorful. The foundation for Freshies Vegetarian Tofu Chili comes from Melodie's college recipe which Chef Ulman has tweaked and fine-tuned. This organic, gluten-free, dairy-free, vegetarian recipe has been a Freshies favorite for 10 years.

12 oz. organic extra firm tofu

1 organic medium yellow onion, diced

4 Serrano chilies, diced

2–15 oz. cans organic tomato sauce

2–15 oz. cans organic diced tomatoes

2 tsp. cumin

1 Tbsp. organic fresh garlic, chopped

1 Tbsp. sea salt

1 tsp. Tabasco sauce

15 oz. can organic kidney beans

3 Tbsp. chili powder

SERVES 6

 EASIEST

Freeze tofu for at least 24 hours, thaw and squeeze all the water out. Crumble tofu into a large pot and add all other ingredients. On medium heat, warm chili until it bubbles. Reduce heat and simmer for 1 hour.

SERVING SUGGESTION:
Top chili with shredded cheddar or pepper jack cheese (no longer dairy-free) and diced red onions. Serve with freshly baked cornbread. Also, enjoy with a glass of wine, such as Madrona Cabernet Franc (El Dorado County)—a local wine on Freshies list.

COTTAGE CHILI

THE COTTAGE AT MIRROR LAKE INN • LAKE PLACID, NEW YORK

Located in the majestic Adirondack Mountains of upstate New York in the Olympic village of Lake Placid, the Mirror Lake Inn is a gracious, traditional inn on the lakeshore. Mirror Lake Inn offers 3 dining options, one being The Cottage with its unique twists on pub-style favorites and special health-conscious dishes.

1 lb. ground beef

1 white onion, chopped

1 green bell pepper, chopped

4–16 oz. cans crushed tomatoes, drained

2–16 oz. cans kidney beans, drained and rinsed

2 Tbsp. chili powder

½ tsp. garlic powder

1 tsp. cumin powder

1 tsp. cayenne pepper

½ tsp. Worcestershire sauce

½ tsp. Tabasco sauce

1 tsp. sugar

½ tsp. salt

SERVES 6

EASIEST

In a large pot, sauté ground beef, onion and green pepper. Drain extra liquid, add all ingredients and boil. Reduce heat and simmer for approximately 30 minutes.

SERVING SUGGESTION:
Ladle into a bread bowl and top with chopped onion, shredded cheddar and Monterey jack cheeses and sour cream.

BAVARIAN GOULASH

THE BAVARIAN RESTAURANT • TAOS SKI VALLEY, NEW MEXICO

Nestled at the base of stunning Kachina Peak above the European-style village of Taos Ski Valley, The Bavarian Lodge and Restaurant offers guests the comfort and charm of an authentic alpine ski chalet amid New Mexico's majestic Sangre de Cristo Mountains. With ski-in/ski-out convenience, while dispensing Old World hospitality, the nationally-acclaimed restaurant serves up Bavarian specialties on its sunny outdoor deck or in its cozy dining room. Secluded but sociable, opulent yet casual, The Bavarian is a magical retreat that brings a taste of the Bavarian Alps to the American Southwest.

1 yellow onion, diced

2 Tbsp. Spanish paprika

2 Tbsp. Hungarian paprika

1 lb. beef, diced

1 lb. pork, diced

1 russet potato, diced

1½ tsp. beef base/bouillon

1½ tsp. pork base/bouillon

8 oz. diced tomatoes

1 bay leaf

2 oz. tomato paste

¼ tsp. ground juniper berry

¼ tsp. granulated garlic

¼ tsp. ground caraway seed

Dash ground thyme

Dash white pepper

Dash dry marjoram

8 cups water

SERVES 8–10

MORE DIFFICULT

In a stock pot with oil, cook onions until caramelized. Add paprika and cook 3–4 minutes. Onions will start to brown. Add beef and pork and cook until water in pan evaporates. Add all other ingredients and stir well. Cover and simmer on low heat for 3 hours. Remove lid and simmer for 20 minutes.

SERVING SUGGESTION:
Pairs well with a French baguette and a Spaten Lager.

CLASSIC CHOPHOUSE CHILI

BEAVER CREEK AND VAIL CHOPHOUSE • CHEF JAY McCARTHY • AVON, COLORADO

For years, Chophouse Corporate Chef Jay McCarthy has worked and traveled the world promoting US Beef. During his travels, Chef McCarthy has judged several chili competitions and, as a result, knows the characteristics of a truly great, award-winning chili. Thus, he refined this recipe spanning trips and beef festivals and continued tweaking the recipe to produce an even more stellar, savory chili. Additionally, Chophouse Chili is gluten-free, dairy-free and, at certain times throughout the year, uses Milagro Ranch grass-fed Piedmontese humanely raised stew beef. As with most chili, this is best prepared a day in advance.

5 lbs. beef, ¼ to ½-inch diced

6 Ancho chili peppers

6 oz. sliced bacon, diced

4 cups yellow onions, diced

8 garlic cloves, peeled

2 Tbsp. chili powder

2 tsp. ground cumin seed

1 tsp. whole oregano leaves

1 tsp. ground coriander

1½ tsp. kosher salt

1¾ cup fire-roasted tomatoes, diced

1 cup green chilies, diced

12 oz. Corona beer

½ cup cilantro, finely chopped

SERVES 8–10

Seed and de-vein the ancho chilies. Soak chilies in hot water until soft, about 15–20 minutes. Remove chilies and puree, add a little of the soaking water. Set aside this thick puree.

In a large pot over medium heat, render diced bacon until crispy, stirring frequently. Remove bacon with a slotted spoon and reserve. In small batches, brown the diced beef on all sides in the bacon fat over medium heat. Remove beef and reserve.

In drippings, sauté onions over medium heat until clear, 3–5 minutes. Stir in all spices until a paste forms, 2–4 minutes. Add garlic and sauté 1–2 minutes. Add tomatoes, green chilies and beer. Return beef, ancho puree, and bacon bits to pot. Simmer uncovered for 1–2 hours or until the diced beef is fork tender.

To finish, add water and/or more beer if chili becomes too thick. Adjust salt and pepper, as necessary. Add cilantro and simmer for a few minutes.

SERVING SUGGESTION:
Serve in a sourdough bowl sprinkled with grated sharp cheddar cheese.

CABIN CHILI

THE CABIN BAR & GRILL • BIG SKY, MONTANA

During the winter season, you can simply ski in to and ski out of The Cabin Bar & Grill via the Silverknife run at Big Sky Resort. What awaits you is this hearty chili that combines chunks of beef and bison with pinto beans, black beans, tomatoes and onions. Owners Curly and Kelly Shea share this secret: the chili is best if made a day before enjoying!

2 lbs. bison meat and beef tenderloin

1 medium onion, diced

¼ cup chili powder

1 tsp. sage

1 tsp. coriander

1 Tbsp. cumin

1 tsp. allspice

Olive oil

2–15 oz. cans diced tomatoes

3–15 oz. cans black beans

2–15 oz. cans pinto beans

15 oz. can of water

SERVES 10–12

Cube meat into bite-size pieces. Place oil, meat, spices and onions in stock pot. Braise on medium-high heat until nicely browned. Add all other ingredients and simmer for at least 2 hours.

SERVING SUGGESTION:
Garnish with grated cheddar cheese, diced onions and sour cream. Also, serve with crackers or tortilla chips.

VENISON CHILI

J-BAR • CHEF RICH HINOJOSA • ASPEN, COLORADO

J-Bar is located inside the Hotel Jerome in Aspen, Colorado. Hotel Jerome has a longstanding tradition of culinary excellence which is showcased in its variety of dining options. The ever-popular J-Bar has been Aspen's favorite watering hole for well over a century—with its authentic saloon ambiance and lively, yet casual, atmosphere. Chef Rich Hinojosa, formerly of J-Bar, serves his scrumptious Venison Chili with accompanying buttermilk cornbread.

¼ cup canola oil

1 lb. venison stew meat, 1-inch cubed

2 medium yellow onions, medium diced

2½ jalapeños, seeded and small diced

¼ cup fresh garlic, minced

2 tsp. dried cumin

⅛ cup smoked paprika

2 tsp. dried oregano

1 tsp. cayenne pepper

1 Tbsp. chili powder

¾ cup dry red wine

¼ cup ruby port

¼ cup brown sugar

32 oz. canned kidney beans, rinsed

32 oz. canned whole plum tomatoes, with liquid

32 oz. water

Salt and pepper to taste

SERVES 6

Heat oil in a stock pot until hot, but not smoking. Add venison meat and brown on all sides. Do not burn. Remove meat from pot and reserve. Sauté onions and jalapeños until translucent, in pot. Add garlic and dry spices, sauté until fragrant, about 45 seconds. Add meat back into pot, and then add the wine and port. Simmer and allow liquid to reduce by 75%.

Add brown sugar and stir until it dissolves. Crush whole tomatoes, roughly, with your hands and add to the pot with beans, water, salt and pepper. Simmer slowly for 2–3 hours, stirring occasionally. Cook until meat is tender. Adjust seasoning to taste with salt, pepper and sugar.

SERVING SUGGESTION:

Ladle chili into an oven-proof soup bowl, melt grated sharp cheddar cheese on top, then add sour cream and diced green onions.

WILD MAINE SHRIMP GUMBO

THE DOWNTOWN GROCERY • CHEF ROGAN LECHTHALER • LUDLOW, VERMONT

The Downtown Grocery creates a divine dining experience with ever-changing specials featuring creative and of-the-moment ingredients. Visit www.SkiTownSoups.com for Chef Lechthaler's Homemade Pork Butt Sausage recipe.

2 lbs. Wild Maine shrimp, shell on

2 lbs. pork sausage, 1-inch sliced

2 lbs. Plew Farm chicken legs and thighs

¼ cup vegetable oil

½ cup all purpose flour

1 Coger's Sugarhouse Garden carrot

1½ medium Prouty Family onions with tops

1 medium Clearbrook Farm red bell pepper

4 Clearbrook Farm celery stalks

8 cups chicken stock

1 cup white rice, cooked

¼ cup Coger's Sugarhouse Garden flat leaf parsley, chopped

Pinch cayenne pepper

Pinch hot Spanish paprika

Salt and pepper

1 quart wood chips

Serves 6

MOST DIFFICULT

Peel skin off chicken legs and thighs, clean meat off the bones. Reserve the bones for stock. Season meat with salt and pepper. Smoke for 40 minutes—use a stove-top smoker and wood chips or use a pot with a colander.

Roast the chicken bones at 375 degrees until golden brown. Chop carrot, ½ of onion, and some celery; sauté in medium pot until caramelized. Add roasted bones and 2 quarts water to cover bones. Simmer for 1 hour. Remove 8 cups chicken stock and cool. With remaining stock, braise the smoked chicken for 90 minutes. Cool the meat and pull by hand into strips.

Peel and clean all but 6 shrimp, saving the shells. In a medium pot, sauté the shrimp shells with ¼ cup vegetable oil until aromatic, stir in flour. Stir roux for about 40 minutes on low heat, until chocolate brown. Meanwhile, dice the other onion (save the tops), celery and bell pepper with no seeds or pith. When roux is dark brown and nutty, add the 8 cups of chicken stock—not smoked stock—slowly. Let roux simmer. Strain to remove shrimp shells—this is the gumbo base.

In a different pot, sauté 1-inch pieces of pork sausage until golden brown. Add diced vegetables and reduce heat. Sweat vegetables for several minutes while stirring. Add pulled, smoked chicken and gumbo base. Season broth with cayenne, hot Spanish paprika, salt and pepper. When ready to serve, season the cleaned shrimp with salt and pepper and add to pot; let heat just long enough to cook shrimp through.

Slice ¾ of the onion tops (or scallion tops) crosswise; the remaining ¼ cut into 3-inch bars, julienne the bars lengthwise and drop into ice water. Peel the bodies of the remaining 6 shrimp, leaving the heads and tail intact. Season the shrimp head with salt and pepper. Grill for garnish.

SERVING SUGGESTION:
In the base of a broad bowl, scoop rice and ladle shrimp gumbo with sausage and smoked chicken over the top. Add chopped parsley and finish with the grilled head-on shrimp and curly onion tops.

PORK & APPLE GOULASH

SKI TIP • CHEF KEVIN MCCOMBS • KEYSTONE, COLORADO

Pork & Apple Goulash was created when Chef Kevin McCombs was researching cuisine for an Eastern European wine dinner. Although goulash is not thought to be fine-dining, it is quintessential European cuisine. Usually prepared as a thick stew, he needed a lighter start to the meal and a dish to pair with a sparkling wine. He started with two staples: sour cream and paprika. He believes these flavors perfectly pair with pork, apples and sparkling wine. The Ski Tip restaurant, located in the Ski Tip Lodge in Keystone, Colorado, was an 1800s stagecoach stop where you can now taste Chef McCombs' fresh, original and dynamic menus.

2 oz. olive oil

2 lbs. pork, cubed

3 cups onions, small diced

1½ cups celery, small diced

1½ cups carrots, small diced

3 Tbsp. shallots, small diced

1 tsp. garlic, minced

1 Tbsp. granulated garlic

2 Tbsp. onion powder

½ tsp. celery salt

1 Tbsp. coriander

1 Tbsp. salt

½ tsp. pepper

2 quarts chicken stock

2 cups apple juice

1 cup sour cream

2 Tbsp. paprika

1 oz. apple cider vinegar

¾ cup cornstarch

5 oz. water

3 granny smith apples, small diced

S ERVES 6–8

MORE DIFFICULT

In a large soup pot, heat oil on medium-high heat. Sear pork on all sides until cooked through. Remove pork from pot and reserve. Add onions, celery, carrots, shallots and garlic to same pot. Sweat until translucent. Return pork to pot along with granulated garlic, onion powder, celery salt, coriander, salt and pepper. Reduce heat to medium-low and continue to cook for approximately 10 minutes. Stir frequently.

Add chicken stock, apple juice, sour cream, paprika and vinegar; increase heat to medium and simmer.

In a small bowl, mix cornstarch with water to make a slurry with no lumps. Whisk in slurry to simmering soup. Add apples and simmer over low heat for approximately 30 minutes. Stir occasionally.

SERVING SUGGESTION:
Serve in a warm bowl with freshly chopped chives and a dollop of sour cream.

MAD RIVER CHILI

THE BASEBOX LODGE • CHEF MICHAEL WITZEL • WAITSFIELD, VERMONT

Great home-style food and the famous Mad River conviviality are hallmarks of the Mad River Glen ski experience. The Basebox Lodge is the hub of activity on the mountain. The cafeteria is famous for its burgers—the meat is brought fresh each day from Mehuron's Market. This same meat is used in the Mad River Chili.

1 lb. Mehuron's Market ground beef, or your local ground beef

4 oz. bacon, medium diced

1 white onion, medium diced

1 green pepper, medium diced

½ Tbsp. garlic, minced

1 Tbsp. maple syrup (or brown sugar)

16 oz. Magic Hat's Single Chair Ale (or another beer)

1 Tbsp. chili powder

1 tsp. dried oregano

1 tsp. dried thyme

½ tsp. ground cumin

½ tsp. dried crushed chilies

½ tsp. black pepper, coarsely ground

16 oz. tomato puree

16 oz. diced tomato

16 oz. kidney beans, drained

1 Tbsp. Tabasco sauce

1 Tbsp. Worcestershire sauce

Salt to taste

SERVES 6–8

MORE DIFFICULT

In a large stock pot, cook ground beef, then drain and set aside. In same pot, render bacon until crisp. Add onions, peppers, garlic and syrup. Lightly caramelize. Deglaze with beer and add spices. Simmer for 5–10 minutes.

Add remaining ingredients, including beef. Simmer for as long as you have—the longer chili cooks, the more flavor develops. Season carefully and add water as moisture evaporates.

SERVING SUGGESTION:

Serve chili topped with shredded sharp cheddar cheese and diced red onions. Accompany with good bread and butter or fresh cornbread.

HOUSE CHILI

BIG SKY RESORT • BIG SKY, MONTANA

From Big Sky Resort, this House Chili recipe is served to tens of thousands of skiers annually.

1 cup canola oil

1 lb. elk meat, ½-inch diced

1 lb. bison meat, ½-inch diced

1 lb. beef, ½-inch diced

1–2 Poblano chilies, small diced

2 Serrano chilies, thinly sliced

2 Ancho chilies, toasted and crushed

1–2 Guajillo chilies, toasted and crushed

2 lbs. yellow onion, small diced

1 cup chili seasonings

⅙ cup beef base

½ Tbsp. Worcestershire sauce

¼ tsp. vanilla paste

2–5# cans water

½–5# can diced tomatoes

½–5# can black beans

½–5# can pinto beans

SERVES 10–12

MOST DIFFICULT

Heat oil on high; sear meat in small batches. Remove meat with a slotted spoon when browned on all sides. Add chili seasonings and cook. Add onions and deglaze pan. Add remaining ingredients, mixing well. Simmer and cook until meat is tender.

CHILI SEASONINGS

1¼ cups dark chili powder

⅛ cup granulated garlic

1½ Tbsp. rubbed sage

1½ Tbsp. ground coriander

⅛ cup ground cumin

¾ Tbsp. ground allspice

⅛ cup kosher salt

Mix all ingredients well, label and store.

SERVING SUGGESTION:
This chili may have a little kick, so serve it with a refreshing beverage.

GOULASH

ALPENHOF BISTRO • TETON VILLAGE, WYOMING

This Austrian eatery is located in the Alpenhof Lodge, the closest hotel to the Jackson Hole tram and lifts. This intimate Teton Village inn exudes genuine Tyrolean charm and comfort. A cozy, welcoming mountain inn with a roaring fire, deep chairs and fabulous food with an atmosphere that welcomes you with open arms and makes you feel instantly at home—an inn that says there is no rush, take your time, relax, and enjoy. Brought to you from Alpenhof Bistro, this delicious, hearty soup will warm you after a cold day on the slopes.

2 lbs. beef chuck, trimmed and cut into ½-inch cubes

2 yellow onions, chopped

2 Tbsp. vegetable oil

2 Tbsp. Hungarian sweet paprika

1 tsp. salt

½ tsp. black pepper, freshly ground

6 oz. can tomato paste

2 garlic cloves, minced

2 cups beef stock

2 medium green bell peppers, cut into ½-inch cubes

3 medium potatoes, peeled and cut into ½-inch cubes

1 tsp. caraway seeds

2 medium carrots, peeled and cut into ½-inch cubes

SERVES 4–6

 EASIEST In a large bowl, mix paprika, salt and pepper together then rub paprika mixture into the meat.

In a Dutch oven, heat oil over medium heat, add onions and cook, stirring occasionally until soft and translucent. Add beef; cook uncovered stirring only once or twice until meat is lightly browned. Stir in caraway and garlic; cook until fragrant, approximately 2 minutes. Add tomato paste, rinsing the can with water to get any remaining paste added to the pot. Stir thoroughly. Add bell peppers, carrots, potatoes and beef stock. Bring to a boil. Reduce heat and simmer, covered until the beef and vegetables are nearly tender, approximately 40 minutes.

SERVING SUGGESTION:
Warm soup bowls in oven and ladle goulash into bowls, top with a dollop of sour cream and serve with a European-style crusty roll.

McGRATH'S GUINNESS STEW

McGRATH'S IRISH PUB • CHEF PATRICK BOANDL • KILLINGTON, VERMONT

When the McGrath family purchased the Inn at Long Trail in 1977, Kyran McGrath transformed the eatery into McGrath's Irish Pub. The Inn began St. Patrick's Day celebrations and introduced McGrath's Guinness Stew. However, not until the mid-1980s, when Guinness on tap was finally brought to Vermont, did the Inn begin to offer McGrath's Guinness Stew daily. A house favorite, owners Murray and Patty McGrath consider it the signature dish at McGrath's Irish Pub at The Inn at Long Trail!

2½ lbs. stewing beef

2 cans Guinness beer

1 quart beef stock

1 Tbsp. Gravy & Gumbo Magic, available online

1¼ lbs. red potatoes, large diced

1 lb. carrots, peeled and large diced

½ Spanish onion, large diced

½ celery bunch, large diced

1 cup corn, frozen

1 cup peas, frozen

½ lb. butter

1 lb. flour

Salt and pepper to taste

SERVES 6–8

MORE DIFFICULT

In a large stew pot on medium heat, brown beef. Drain fat. Add Guinness, beef stock and Gravy Magic. Boil and reduce heat to simmer for 2 hours. Add potatoes, carrots, celery and onions; continue to simmer for 1 hour.

While vegetables are cooking, melt butter in a separate pot. Add flour to make a roux, let roux cook on very low heat until it has a nutty aroma. Set aside.

Add frozen corn and peas to stew; continue boiling for 30 minutes. Drain stew liquid into a second pot, reserving the beef and vegetables in the first pot. Add roux to the broth and heat until it thickens. Add enough roux to make a gravy consistency. Add gravy back to beef and vegetables and stir over low heat for 10 minutes. Season with salt and pepper to taste.

SERVING SUGGESTION:
Serve stew with French bread or homemade Irish soda bread.

BEEF & BARLEY STEW

MERRY-GO-ROUND RESTAURANT • CHEF DE CUISINE PHIL HOUSE • ASPEN, COLORADO

Located mid-mountain at the top of the Exhibition lift on Aspen Highlands, the Merry-Go-Round restaurant continues to boast the largest outdoor deck in the Roaring Fork Valley. This 1960s era eatery claimed the 2011 SoupSköl trophy, a joyous soup-cooking contest judged by the public to determine which Aspen restaurant has the best soup in town. This competition is a part of Aspen's Annual Wintersköl Celebration.

4 Tbsp. extra virgin olive oil

2 lbs. beef stew meat, 1-inch diced

1½ cups yellow onion, ¼-inch diced

1½ cups carrots, ¼-inch diced

1 cup celery, ¼-inch diced

2 garlic cloves, finely minced

1 bunch fresh thyme

1 bay leaf

1 Tbsp. sherry vinegar

10 cups beef stock

3 plum tomatoes, 1-inch diced

¾ cup pearl barley, toasted until golden brown

2 Tbsp. fresh oregano, roughly chopped

Salt and pepper to taste

SERVES 8–10

MORE DIFFICULT

Season the beef stew meat liberally with salt and freshly-cracked black pepper. Sear the beef stew meat in a thick bottomed pot with the extra virgin olive oil. You may need to do this in small batches, depending on the size of the pot. Once the beef is nicely browned, remove from the pot.

In the same pot, add vegetables and cook for 2 minutes, or until onions become slightly translucent. Add garlic, thyme and bay leaf. Cook for 1–2 minutes, ensuring that the garlic doesn't brown (it will make the stew bitter). Add sherry vinegar and allow it to boil off. Add beef broth and tomatoes, then cook until beef is just starting to become tender, about 1 hour.

Add barley and cook until barley is tender. Check the stew for seasoning. Add salt and pepper, as necessary.

SERVING SUGGESTION:
Just before serving, add chopped oregano to stew and ladle into a bowl.

SMOKED BRISKET CHILI

THE BLACKSMITH RESTAURANT • CHEF GAVIN MCMICHAEL • BEND, OREGON

The Blacksmith Restaurant is Bend, Oregon's culinary tribute to the wholesome cooking that fueled the journey west along the Oregon Trail. The restaurant features New Ranch Cuisine, a food direction that blends the best of the West with the bold flavors of southwestern style cooking, adding the sophistication and presentation of European cuisine. "New Ranch Cuisine is what happens when a cowboy strikes oil on his ranch," says Executive Chef and Co-Owner Gavin McMichael.

4 dried red chilies or pasilla chilies, stemmed and seeded

2½ cups water

2 Tbsp. garlic, chopped

1 large yellow onion, chopped

1½ lbs. smoked beef brisket, shredded

1 Tbsp. dried oregano

1 tsp. dried sage

1 Tbsp. smoked paprika

2 cups chili puree

½ tsp. cornstarch or masa flour

2–15 oz. cans diced tomatoes with liquid

6 oz. can tomato paste

½ cup Worcestershire sauce

2 Tbsp. molasses

2 cups of water

1 cup beef broth

2 cans red kidney beans

1 bay leaf

1 Tbsp. cider vinegar

Salt to taste

Corn tortillas for frying

Canola oil for frying

SERVES 6–8

For the chili puree, boil 2½ cups water on the stove. While water is heating, lightly toast the chilies in a 350 degree oven for 2–3 minutes. Place toasted chilies in a bowl and pour hot water over them. Soak until soft and water is just warm. Blend water and chili mixture in blender until smooth. Set aside.

In a large pot, sweat garlic and onions until translucent. Add ½ lb. of smoked brisket and oregano, sage, and smoked paprika. Cook, stirring constantly, for another 2–3 minutes; add chili puree. Mix and cook for 2–3 more minutes. Add canned tomatoes, tomato paste, Worcestershire sauce, beef broth, and molasses. Combine the cornstarch or masa flour with 1 Tbsp. of water and mix until smooth, and then add it to the chili mixture and blend well. Add 2 cups water, bay leaf and kidney beans. Reduce heat to medium-low and cook for 45–60 minutes at a low simmer. Chili will thicken. Add vinegar and remove bay leaf.

Cut tortillas into thin strips and fry until crisp in ½ cup or more of hot canola oil, about 375 degrees.

Over medium-high heat, warm remaining 1 lb. shredded, smoked brisket in a covered skillet with ½ cup of water until moist.

SERVING SUGGESTION:

Ladle chili into a bowl and pile-on the warmed brisket, top with crispy tortilla strips, crumbled queso blanco cheese, and finish with cumin crema.
Visit SkiTownSoups.com for Chef Gavin's Cumin Crema recipe.

VENISON CHILI

THE JUNCTION RESTAURANT AND SALOON • SNOWSHOE, WEST VIRGINIA

The Junction is home-style cooking at its best! Located in the village, The Junction Restaurant and Saloon is also Snowshoe's most unique dining experience. When you walk into The Junction, it's like taking a step back in time: rail yard and logging memorabilia from Cass, West Virginia, adorns the walls giving you a look inside a turn of the century train station and logging mill.

2 lbs. ground venison

12 oz. can black beans

12 oz. can red kidney beans

5 oz. can tomato juice

1 Tbsp. dry mustard

1 Tbsp. chili powder

1 Tbsp. hot sauce

½ Tbsp. sugar

1 Tbsp. salt

1 cup onions, diced

½ cup garlic, chopped

½ cup red wine

2 Tbsp. beef base

1 Tbsp. cumin

12 oz. can tomato puree

12 oz. can diced tomatoes

SERVES 4–6

In a heavy-bottomed pot, cook venison. Remove venison. Drain excess fat from pot; add garlic and onions. Sauté until golden, then return venison to pot and stir.

Add all remaining ingredients. Boil, then reduce heat and simmer 1 hour.

SERVING SUGGESTION:
Serve hot with shredded cheese and diced onions.

Kelly Liken

Owner and Executive Chef of Restaurant Kelly Liken, Kelly Liken is one of Colorado's most promising and influential young chefs. Her mother was an outstanding cook, constantly exploring new recipes and seeking out fresh products at the local farmers market—which is undoubtedly what led Kelly to develop her love for cooking beginning in high school. "From the moment I stepped foot into a professional kitchen, I knew it was where I wanted to be . . . it was like an epiphany," Kelly recalls.

In 2004, she opened Restaurant Kelly Liken at the entrance to Vail Village, one of the state's most sophisticated dining destinations, where the restaurant's cosmopolitan décor and progressive American cuisine mirror the owner/chef's personality.

Her menu reflects the incredible bounty of Colorado and a reverence for the seasons. She explains, "Colorado has an amazing selection of ingredients you can get at the local farmer's market including bison, elk, wild porcini mushrooms grown on the local hillsides and turnips and potatoes grown at 8,300 feet above sea level—all truly divine." To accommodate her heartfelt market-driven philosophy, Kelly nurtures close relationships with small family farmers, ranchers and artisanal food producers.

A James Beard nominee for Best Chef: Southwest (2009, 2010 and 2011), Kelly has garnered national recognition for her creativity in the kitchen as well as her commitment to and passion for her craft. She was featured in *Bon Appétit*, 2008 "Women Chefs: The Next Generation," as one of the emerging female chefs to watch in the country and has appeared on the Food Network's Iron Chef America. She was also a contestant on Bravo's Season 7 of Top Chef D.C.

Chef Liken and her husband generously support local charities dedicated to improving the quality of education in Colorado, and Kelly continues working in partnership with the Vail Valley Foundation's Youth Foundation on the Sowing Seeds program.

See page 15 for Chef Kelly Liken's Spiced Rum Spiked Acorn Squash Soup with Gorgonzola and Toasted Pecans.

Kevin McCombs

In Keystone, Colorado, Executive Chef Kevin McCombs makes the Ski Tip kitchen his own. Although he was raised in Tennessee, Chef McCombs has been calling Colorado home since 2003. The pursuit of a degree and a career in the culinary arts led him to the great state of Colorado. "I cherish my southern upbringing but even more than cooking, I love where I live." Chef Kevin began to hone the skills necessary to expand his culinary boundaries at Colorado Mountain College in Keystone. At the Ski Tip, Chef Kevin states, "With a nightly rotating menu of beef, fish, game and seasonal fare, the creativity flows and the imaginative combinations are endless."

See page 126 for Chef Kevin McCombs' Pork and Apple Goulash.

Eric Gruber

Chef Eric Gruber brings more than two decades of culinary knowledge and experience to Shore Lodge, Whitetail Club and The Cove in McCall, Idaho. A graduate of the Scottsdale Culinary Institute, Chef Gruber has worked at several 4-star, 4-diamond establishments. He has served as Executive Chef at the resort properties since September 2008. His philosophy of building menus around seasonal and regional ingredient-driven cuisine is showcased most notably at The Narrows, Shore Lodge's fine-dining restaurant. Locally sourced products like grass-fed lamb from Hailey, Idaho, with mountain huckleberries picked fresh in McCall, are highlights of the menu.

Chef Eric serves on the advisory board of BehindTheKnife.com, a website about chefs' arsenals of tools and the stories behind them. He is also a frequent guest on local morning TV talk shows throughout Idaho.

See page 48 for Chef Eric Gruber's Butternut Squash and Apple Soup.

HEARTY SOUPS

DEEP WINTER CARAMELIZED CREAM OF ONION SOUP
with Rogue Creamery Smokey Blue Cheese

KETCHUM GRILL • CHEFS SCOTT MASON AND ANNE MASON • KETCHUM, IDAHO

This soup, richer than many of the other popular soups served at Ketchum Grill, satisfies like none other, especially around the holidays. It has become a seasonal favorite! The soup is extraordinarily great with Rogue Creamery Smokey Blue Cheese, as well as imported gorgonzola or Papillion Roquefort.

½ cup unsalted butter

6 large yellow onions, peeled and julienned

1 tsp. ground white pepper

3 tsp. dried thyme

½ cup all-purpose flour

3 cups dry sherry

1 gallon home-made chicken stock, low sodium

1 quart heavy cream

2 Tbsp. kosher salt

2 Tbsp. lemon juice

2 tsp. Tabasco sauce

3 twists black pepper, freshly ground

4 oz. Rogue Creamery Smokey Blue Cheese

Fresh thyme

SERVES 8–10

In a heavy bottom pot, melt butter and add onions. Sauté over medium heat until onions are caramelized. This may take up to 30 minutes. Stir the onions often to keep from burning. Stir in white pepper and thyme. Add flour and mix thoroughly with onions. Add sherry and cook until thick. Stir in chicken stock and bring to boil. Reduce heat and cook for 5 minutes.

Add cream, salt, lemon juice, black pepper and Tabasco. Bring soup to a boil. Adjust seasoning, if needed.

SERVING SUGGESTION:
Serve hot, garnished with crumbles of smokey blue cheese and freshly chopped thyme. Also, pair with a glass of Trimbach Cuvee Frederick Emile Riesling or Alois Lageder Pinot Grigio.

BEET GAZPACHO

TABERNASH TAVERN • CHEF ALBERTO SAPIEN • TABERNASH, COLORADO

Carol and Joe Morales, owners of Morales Farms, experimentally planted many beet plants one year, wondering if they would grow in Grand County, Colorado. Come harvest time, they had a surplus, to say the least. When asked, Chef Alberto Sapien was thrilled to accept some. It was the winter of beets at Tabernash Tavern, and Beet Gazpacho was created out of necessity. This recipe is delightfully gluten-free.

3 large Morales Farm red beets, roasted—
½ chopped into large chunks, ½ small diced

8 whole peppercorns

2 bay leaves

1 Granny Smith apple, peeled, cored—
½ chopped into large chunks, ½ small diced

1 cucumber, peeled and seeded—½ chopped
into large chunks, ½ small diced

½ cup orange juice

3 Tbsp. champagne vinegar

½ yellow bell pepper, small diced

2 Morales Farm scallions, thinly sliced

1 oz. Morales Farm chervil—½ chopped,
½ sprigs for garnish

4 Tbsp. sour cream

SERVES 4

Place halved beets in deep roasting pan with bay leaves and peppercorns; add warm water until beets are covered. Cover with foil; slowly roast in a 325 degree oven for 3 hours or until "fork tender". Drain water. Cool slightly and peel beets while still warm—the peel should fall right off. Cool completely. This can be done a day ahead and beets kept refrigerated.

Combine large chopped and roasted beets, large chopped apples and cucumbers, orange juice and vinegar. Puree in blender until very smooth. Place puree in large bowl and add small diced and roasted beets, small diced apples, cucumbers and yellow bell peppers, scallions and chopped chervil. Mix well and chill.

SERVING SUGGESTION:

Pour soup into 4 chilled soup bowls. Add a dollop of sour cream. Finish with sprig of chervil. Accompany this soup with toasted garlic french bread and a glass of dry German Riesling.

PASTA E FAGIOLI

ALLRED'S RESTAURANT • TELLURIDE, COLORADO

Allred's General Manager Mario Petillo invites you to Telluride's flagship restaurant at the top of the gondola—a restaurant which offers one of the most unique dining experiences in North America. Enjoy the atmosphere and service at this elegant Italian restaurant and the best restaurant views in Telluride! Pasta e Fagioli, a traditional Italian meatless dish, translates to Pasta with Beans.

15 oz. can cannellini beans

1 garlic clove, diced

A few celery stalks, diced

1 medium onion, diced

Parmesan cheese

8 oz. pasta of your choice

Pepper, freshly ground

Sea salt

3 Tbsp. olive oil

S ERVES 4

In a large soup pot over medium-high heat, sauté garlic, onions and celery in olive oil. Add cold water and boil for 15 minutes. Add cannellini beans and pasta. Cook for 10 minutes, then let it rest for a few minutes. Add parmesan cheese, freshly ground pepper, sea salt and a touch of olive oil.

SERVING SUGGESTION:
Mario merely states, "Buon Appetito ...Ciao"!

CELERY & LEEK POTAGE
with Glazed Short Rib, Lentil Du Puy & Tuscan Oil

LARKSPUR RESTAURANT • CHEF THOMAS SALAMUNOVICH • VAIL, COLORADO

The secret to Larkspur's consistency is its high caliber of staff, widely considered "the special Larkspur family." The whole team is responsible and enjoys the opportunity to provide every guest with a wonderful dining experience. For Larkspur's Glazed Short Rib recipe, visit SkiTownSoups.com.

4 Tbsp. olive oil

3 lbs. (2-3) leeks, white and green parts, thinly sliced

1 ½ oz. (1 head) garlic, minced

2 ½ lbs. (2 ½) yellow onions, thinly sliced

4 ½ lbs. potatoes, thinly sliced

2 gallons chicken stock

½ oz. (1 bunch) thyme

5 bay leaves

1 Tbsp. peppercorns

2 lbs. celery, rough chopped

6 oz. (2 bunches) parsley, picked

3 oz. arugula

½ gallon heavy cream

2 ½ lbs. (1 ½ quarts) celery, juiced

2 lbs. glazed short rib, prepared and cubed

SERVES 10–12

MOST DIFFICULT

Heat olive oil on medium heat in a large pot. Add onions, leeks and garlic, reduce heat to low and sweat onions until completely soft, about 10 minutes. Add sliced potatoes and sweat for 10 minutes. Add chicken stock, bay leaves, thyme and peppercorns. Simmer for 20 minutes. Add cream and simmer for 15 minutes. Transfer into a large bowl and place over an ice bath. Stir soup base until chilled.

Boil a large pot of salted water. Add chopped celery and cook until completely tender. Remove celery and place in ice water to cool. Add parsley and arugula to boiling salt water; cook until tender. Remove greens and place in ice water to cool. Once all are cooled, strain. In a blender, puree blanched greens with soup base until smooth. Add salt and pepper to taste. Thin soup with juiced celery to a consistency that barely coats the back of a spoon.

LENTIL DU PUY

Olive oil

2 lbs. dry du puy lentils, French green lentils

1 yellow onion, small diced

1 large carrot, small diced

3 celery stalks, small diced

2 quarts chicken stock

Salt and pepper to taste

In a sauce pot, heat 1 Tbsp. olive oil and cook onions until tender, about 7 minutes. Add lentils and chicken stock; cover and simmer until lentils are soft, about 25 minutes. Pour into a large bowl and cool over ice bath. In another sauce pot, heat 1 Tbsp. olive oil and sweat carrots and celery until soft, about 7 minutes. Cool and mix vegetables together. Adjust seasoning.

To assemble, heat soup over low heat, stirring every 5 minutes. Heat lentils in sauce pot over low heat—incorporate some short rib sauce (or 1 cup reduction from Larkspur's recipe). Warm short rib cubes at 300 degree with some short rib sauce (or 2 cups of reduction from Larkspur's recipe). Baste short rib every 10 minutes until hot, about 30 minutes.

SERVING SUGGESTION:
Place lentils in a bowl with short rib cubes on top, then garnish with finely diced celery, extra virgin olive oil and sea salt. Finish with hot soup.

SOUTHWESTERN BLACK BEAN & SWEET POTATO SOUP

UPTOWN FARE • PARK CITY, UTAH

The "Deer Valley Difference" has prompted readers of SKI Magazine to name Deer Valley Resort the #1 ski resort in North America. It's the smiling staff members who carry your skis from the car to the snow. Its bottomless powder turns in the aspen forest. It's the limited number of daily lift tickets sold so that you spend your precious vacation time actually skiing. It's the complimentary overnight ski storage so that you never have to struggle home with cumbersome gear. It's grooming so fine you could practically roll a coin down the corduroy grooves. It's also evident in little things like the grated cheese, green onions and sour cream.

4–16 oz. cans black beans, rinsed

2 large sweet potatoes, diced

Olive oil

1½ large onions, diced

4 garlic cloves, minced

2 red or yellow (not green) peppers, diced

2 jalapeno peppers, diced

2 hot or mild peppers (such as Armenian or Poblano), diced

1 chipotle pepper in adobo sauce, finely chopped with some sauce

3–15 oz. cans diced tomatoes

1 tsp. ground cumin

4 Tbsp. chili powder

1 tsp. dried oregano (Mexican, preferably)

1 tsp. dried coriander

Serves 10–12

EASIEST

Heat oil in a large pot; add onions, peppers, garlic and spices. Cook until vegetables are tender, then add remaining ingredients. Add water if soup is too thick. Cook approximately 30 minutes until sweet potatoes are tender. Add salt and pepper to taste; if you want some heat, add a pinch of cayenne pepper.

SERVING SUGGESTION:
Use sour cream and chopped cilantro for topping this hearty soup.

FIVE ONION SOUP

FORMERLY OF ST. BERNARD'S • CHEF MATT BARRIGAR • BRIGHTON, UTAH

Chef Matt Barrigar created the Five Onion Soup for St. Bernard's Restaurant before moving his culinary talent elsewhere in Utah. St. Bernard's is located inside the Inn at Solitude and continues to inspire your palette with local, fresh ingredients served fireside next to breathtaking views of Solitude's mountain.

2 quarts yellow onions, julienned

3 cups red onions, julienned

1 cup shallots, julienned

1 cup pearl onions, halved

¼ lb. unsalted butter

½ cup garlic cloves, thinly sliced

⅓ cup flour

1 cup brandy

2 quarts beef stock

¼ cup fresh thyme, chopped

4 bay leaves

3 Tbsp. soy sauce

2 Tbsp. Worcestershire sauce

3 Tbsp. sherry vinegar

Salt and pepper to taste

SERVES 6–8

MORE DIFFICULT Melt butter in heavy soup pot over low heat. Add all onions and shallots; cook over low heat, stirring often, until dark brown (about 30–40 minutes).

Add garlic and flour. Cook until flour is dissolved (about 2 minutes). Add brandy. Cook for approximately two minutes, then add stock, thyme, bay leaves, soy sauce, Worcestershire, sherry vinegar and seasoning.

Bring to a slow boil, and reduce heat. Simmer for at least an hour. Adjust seasoning.

SERVING SUGGESTION:
Ladle into heavy, oven-safe soup bowls. Top with toasted baguette slices and a 50/50 mix of Gruyere and Emmenthal cheese. Top with sliced green onions. Broil until cheese is completely melted and slightly browned. Serve hot.

BUTTERNUT SQUASH & CARROT SOUP

LAKE LOUISE SKI AREA • CHEF BRUCE EDMONDSON • LAKE LOUISE, ALBERTA

Along with delicious on-the-mountain dining options, Lake Louise offers spectacular scenery with uniquely beautiful terrain that is both vast and varied. The wilderness viewed out of the lodges and chalets is pristine and inspirational. Located in the heart of majestic, historic Banff National Park, Lake Louise skiing is truly legendary and offers world-class terrain.

¼ cup butter

5 large carrots, diced

3 celery stalks, diced

2 Tbsp. garlic, minced

1 large onion, diced

2 medium butternut squash, peeled, seeded and chopped

1 tsp. cinnamon

20 cups water

4 cups cream

4 Tbsp. cornstarch

¼ cup honey

SERVES 12

 EASIEST In a large pot, bring water and ¾ of the butternut squash to a boil, reduce heat and simmer until squash starts to break down.

In a separate large soup pot, sweat garlic, carrots, onions, celery, the remaining butternut squash and butter. When onions are clear and celery is tender, add squash and water mixture, cinnamon, cream and honey. Simmer to a gentle, rolling boil.

In a small bowl, make a slurry: mix cornstarch with enough water so it coats the back of a spoon. Add the slurry to thicken the soup.

SERVING SUGGESTION:
Using equal parts sour cream and whipping cream, make a Crème Fraiche for garnishing each bowl. Sprinkle finely-chopped parsley over Crème Fraiche.

CHICKEN TORTILLA SOUP

THE LAST STEEP BAR AND GRILL • CRESTED BUTTE, COLORADO

A family-owned-and-operated restaurant in the heart of historic downtown Crested Butte, Colorado, The Last Steep serves a variety of specialties with a somewhat southern flare due to the family's Kansas City, Missouri, connection. The restaurant is named after owners Kevin, Sean and Sarah Hartigan's favorite North Face ski run at Crested Butte Mountain Resort and Ski Area.

½ yellow onion, diced

¼ green bell pepper, diced

2 Tbsp. green chili, diced

2 Tbsp. canned roasted red peppers, diced

1½ tomatoes, diced

1 Tbsp. garlic, minced

½ cup mushrooms, sliced (optional)

1 quart tomato sauce

1 gallon chicken stock

1 gallon water mixed with 4 oz. chicken base

¼ cilantro bunch, chopped

¼ lime, juiced

2 Tbsp. Cholula sauce

⅛ cup corn

1 Tbsp. chipotle powder

3 cups chicken, cooked and pulled

Salt and pepper to taste

2 cups tortilla chips

SERVES 10–12

MORE DIFFICULT

In a large pot with a small amount of oil, sauté onions, peppers, chili, tomatoes, garlic and mushrooms. Add remaining ingredients. Boil and adjust seasoning with salt and pepper.

SERVING SUGGESTION:
Garnish soup with chopped parsley and tortilla chips.

HUNGARIAN MUSHROOM SOUP

DENO'S MOUNTAIN BISTRO • WINTER PARK, COLORADO

Introduced to Deno's Mountain Bistro by former employee "Alaskan Bob" Halverson, Hungarian Mushroom Soup was so popular it became a permanent fixture on the menu.

5 cups mushrooms, thinly sliced

1 cup yellow onions, thinly sliced

2 tsp. olive oil

2 large shallots, thinly sliced

4 garlic cloves, finely chopped

1 cup sour cream

4 cups water

3 vegetable bouillon cubes

½ cup sherry

2 cups milk

1 cup heavy cream

6 Tbsp. butter

4 Tbsp. flour

2 tsp. salt

1 tsp. white pepper

2 tsp. paprika

SERVES 10–12

On medium heat, melt 2 Tbsp. butter. Add flour and stir continuously until mixture is brown in color. Remove from heat and keep warm.

On low heat, warm olive oil in a small sauté pan. Add shallots and garlic; sauté until deep golden brown. Set aside.

In a large sauce pan, melt remaining butter on medium heat. Sauté onions until soft. Stir in mushrooms and wilt. Add shallot and garlic mixture. Deglaze with sherry and reduce by half. Add milk, water, cream, sour cream and bouillon cubes. Boil mixture and add roux (flour-butter mixture). Stir to incorporate. Boil and reduce to a simmer for 8–10 minutes. Season with salt and white pepper to taste. Shake paprika through a fine strainer and stir into mixture.

SERVING SUGGESTION:
Ladle soup in bowls and garnish with chopped chives or scallions.

BEER CHEESE & JALAPEÑO SAUSAGE SOUP

FULL BELLY DELI • CHEF TOM MARRIN • TRUCKEE, CALIFORNIA

With his training in fine dining, Chef and Owner Tom Marrin blows away the notion of what a deli sandwich should be while delivering modern, seasonal twists on traditional Mexican/Southwestern food at Full Belly Deli. In his short time on the local culinary scene, Tom's contribution to Truckee/Tahoe has been kindly recognized: Silver Medal for Best Pairing at the 2008 Autumn Food and Wine Festival, North Lake Tahoe's Best Deli, 2010 Truckee Chili Cook-off Grand Prize and People's Choice Winner.

2 lbs. Carson City Sausage Factory Jalapeño-Cheddar Bratwurst, halved and sliced (or your favorite un-cooked sausage)

2 celery stalks, diced

2 large leeks, white and pale parts, diced

1 bunch Sierra Valley Farm organic carrots, diced

2 Tbsp. canola oil

3 Tbsp. unsalted butter

2 large Sierra Valley Farm organic shallots, diced

4 cups chicken stock or broth

4 cups half and half

12 oz. domestic lager (preferably Pabst Blue Ribbon)

2 lbs. sharp cheddar cheese, grated

2 tsp. Tabasco sauce

1 tsp. dry mustard

2 bay leaves

½ cup all purpose flour

Kosher salt and ground black pepper to taste

SERVES 6–8

MORE DIFFICULT

Heat canola oil and brown sliced sausages in 4-quart Dutch oven on medium-high heat, approximately 8–10 minutes. Remove sausages from pot and set aside.

Add butter, celery, leeks, shallots and carrots to pot and stir. Scrape bottom of pot to deglaze. Sweat vegetables until soft, approximately 7–9 minutes. Reduce heat to low-medium and sprinkle flour over vegetables. Stir well and cook for 3 minutes. Stir occasionally.

Add beer to vegetable/flour mixture and stir well. As mixture starts to thicken, slowly add half and half and chicken stock. Simmer and stir occasionally, approximately 5 minutes.

Stir in dry mustard and bay leaves. Slowly add cheddar cheese in handfuls. Stir each until cheese melts. When soup is smooth, add Tabasco and salt and pepper to taste.

SERVING SUGGESTION:
Garnish soup with a soft baked pretzel, cubed. If you want to make your own baked soft pretzel bites, you can find Full Belly Deli's recipe at www.SkiTownSoups.com. Also, top the soup with sliced green onions or chives.

CIOPPINO

JOHN PAUL LODGE • HUNTSVILLE, UTAH

During the winter season, John Paul Lodge offers dining on two floors, including the wrap-around patio on the main level. With breathtaking views, a four-sided fireplace, oak and Italian marble tables with cozy, upholstered chairs and hearty Italian specialties, John Paul Lodge has become "the place to be!" The lodge, which is located at 8,900 feet, is accessible via the John Paul high-speed quad chair lift.

28 oz. can diced tomatoes, in juice

¼ cup tomato paste

2 green onions, chopped

1 large roasted green bell pepper, diced

1 Tbsp. garlic, minced

1 Tbsp. fresh basil, chopped

¼ tsp. thyme

4 oz. red wine

2 dashes Tabasco sauce

2 tsp. black pepper

1 lb. Manila clams, scrubbed

2 bay leaves

1½ lbs. cod fillets, cut into 2-inch chunks

1 lb. (26–30) shrimp

5 cups fish stock

1 lb. black mussels scrubbed and de-bearded

2 Tbsp. lobster base

1 large yellow onion, diced

½ cup carrots, diced

½ cup celery, diced

3 Tbsp. olive oil

SERVES 8–10

MOST DIFFICULT

In a soup kettle, sweat onions, celery and carrots with olive oil until translucent. Deglaze with red wine. Add garlic, green onions, green peppers, tomatoes and paste. Add fish stock and lobster base and bring to a boil. Add remaining herbs and all seafood. Simmer for 1 hour.

Discard any clams and mussels that do not open. Adjust seasoning with salt, pepper and Tabasco sauce.

SERVING SUGGESTION:
For visual appeal, place a sprig of thyme atop Cioppino.

PHEASANT SOUP

ALEXANDER'S • OLYMPIC VALLEY, CALIFORNIA

At an elevation of 8,200 feet, Alexander's at High Camp in Squaw Valley is accessible only via the aerial cable car (North America's largest) which ascends two thousand vertical feet to the mountain top complex. Squaw Valley hosted the 1960 Winter Olympics and is internationally renowned for terrain that spans 3,600 skiable acres, six peaks and 30 chairlifts, all of which ranges from an expansive mountaintop beginner area to unrivaled expert steeps, trees and bowls. Recently, Squaw Valley combined with Alpine Meadows bringing the two ski resorts under common ownership. Skiers and riders can now access 6,000 skiable acres, 43 lifts and 270+ trails at Squaw Valley and Alpine Meadows.

1 cup smoked pheasant, cooked

½ cup celery

½ cup yellow onion

½ cup carrot

⅓ cup water

⅓—½ cup corn kernels

⅙ cup butter

⅙ cup flour

4 cups heavy cream

1¼ Tbsp. Sriracha

1¼ Tbsp. Liquid Smoke

¼ cup wild rice, cooked

¼ cup apple juice

Kosher salt to taste

Freshly ground black pepper to taste

SERVES 2–4

 MORE DIFFICULT

Roast corn in a 350 degree oven until golden brown. Pull pheasant meat off bones, set meat aside and reserve bones. Dice celery, onions and carrots and set aside. Reserve peels, tops and ends from vegetables. Boil bones, water, tops, ends and peels from vegetables to make stock. Boil for 30–60 minutes. Strain and set aside. Sauté diced vegetables in melted butter in a large sauce pot until translucent. Add flour and cook for 3–4 minutes, until a roux forms. Add cream, apple juice and stock, then boil.

Add smoke, seasonings, sriracha, rice, corn and meat. Simmer for approximately 30 minutes to incorporate flavors.

SERVING SUGGESTION:
Top with sweet potato curls and pumpkin seed oil. Serve with saltine crackers.

ROSEMARY CHICKEN & MUSHROOM SOUP

LOULA'S CAFÉ • CHEF SHAUN MCCOLLUM • WHITEFISH, MONTANA

The winters in Whitefish, Montana, are longer than the summers, so a nice warm bowl of soup is always a "HOT" item. Whether it is Zucchini Bisque or Chicken Dumpling, the locals have literally been eating up the variety of outstanding daily soups at LouLa's Café. Chef Shaun McCollum created this soup many years ago, and it continues to be a favorite of the customers and the staff. Next time it is snowing outside, try this comfort soup. It is a treat for all your senses and a perfect way to warm up before or after a long day in the snow. It will bring LouLa's of Whitefish into your very own kitchen!

4 cups chicken stock

3 sprigs of fresh rosemary

½ lemon

1 bay leaf

2–3 chicken breasts

3 Tbsp. canola oil or butter

1 cup carrots, diced

2 cups onions, diced

1 cup celery, diced

1 Tbsp. garlic, minced

3 cups button mushrooms, sliced

½ cup dry white wine

1 cup all purpose flour

3 cups milk

1 Tbsp. Worcestershire sauce

¼ cup heavy cream

Salt and pepper to taste

SERVES 6–8

MORE DIFFICULT

In a medium sauce pan, add first five ingredients and cook at medium-low heat, covered. Cook until chicken is done and tender. Remove chicken breasts and cool, until workable with bare hands. Dice chicken into bite-sized pieces and set aside. Strain cooking liquid and reserve.

In a large stock pot over medium-high heat, heat oil or butter. Add carrots, onions, celery and garlic plus two pinches of salt and one pinch of pepper. Sauté until vegetables start to caramelize. Stirring often, add white wine and mushrooms, cooking until wine reduces by half. Add flour, stirring constantly, until incorporated. Add milk and continuously stir until milk heats and mixture starts to thicken. Add diced chicken, Worcestershire sauce and a pinch of salt and pepper. Reduce heat, simmer and stir occasionally.

If soup is too thick, thin with reserved chicken stock mixture—remember you'll still add heavy cream. Once soup is the correct consistency, add cream and heat for 5 minutes.

Remove bay leaf and adjust seasoning with salt and pepper to taste, prior to removing it from the stove.

SERVING SUGGESTION:

Ladle soup into bowls and garnish with a sprig of fresh rosemary and a big slice of warm artisan bread. Also, pair with a glass of Pinot Noir and a slice of LouLa's Famous Huckleberry Peach Pie.

DUNGENESS CRAB & COCONUT MILK SOUP

ARAXI RESTAURANT + BAR • CHEF JAMES WALT • WHISTLER, BRITISH COLUMBIA

Chef James Walt likes subtle, ethnic flavors, such as he's infused in this excellent soup in which the curry sets off, but doesn't overwhelm, the flavor of the crab. The restaurant sometimes serves a crab spring roll to dip in this soup. And, the recipe works with lobster as well: cook the lobster for 8 minutes in the stock and make the rest of the dish the same way you would with the crab. Chef Walt gives this tip: chilling the live shellfish in the freezer for 20–30 minutes before you begin makes it easier to handle.

10 cups fish or chicken stock

2 lbs. live Dungeness crabs

2 Tbsp. grapeseed oil

2 medium onions, minced

½-inch piece ginger, peeled and minced

2 red jalapeño peppers, seeded and minced

1½ Tbsp. mild curry powder

1 Tbsp. ground turmeric

2½ cups coconut milk

2 limes, juiced

2 Tbsp. fresh cilantro leaves or chives, chopped

SERVES 10–12

In a large pot fitted with a lid, bring the stock to a boil on high heat. Add crab, reduce heat to medium, cover and cook for 12 minutes. Using tongs, transfer crab to a large bowl, placing it shell side down; refrigerate for 30 minutes or until chilled. Strain the stock through a fine-mesh sieve, discard the solids and set aside.

Heat the grapeseed oil in a medium sauce pan on medium-low heat. Add onions, ginger and jalapeño peppers; sauté until very soft and fragrant, about 10 minutes. Add curry powder and turmeric and cook 3 minutes more to release the flavors.

Add strained stock and coconut milk; increase heat to medium-high and boil, then reduce heat to low and simmer for 15–20 minutes. Remove from heat, stir in lime juice. Season with salt and set aside.

To clean the crab, hold the base of the crab with one hand and lift off the shell with the other. Discard the shell. With a spoon, gently scrape away and discard the gills on both sides (the off-white bits between the legs), the intestine and other innards that run down the back and fill the cavity. Rinse the crab under cold water. Break the body in half and twist off the legs. Using a nutcracker or a mallet, crack the legs. Remove the meat with a fork or a pick, then crack the body sections and remove the meat from those, as well.

Heat the soup over medium heat, then add the crabmeat.

SERVING SUGGESTION:

Ladle soup into warmed bowls; garnish with cilantro or chives. Natural wine pairings are an Alsatian blend like JoieFarm's Noble Blend or Mosel Riesling.

RED LENTIL COCONUT SOUP WITH LIME

BONELLI'S BISTRO • KALISPELL, MONTANA

Bonelli's Bistro is a brightly colored Italian/Mediterranean bistro in the heart of downtown Kalispell, Montana. The restaurant is proud to offer their customers the finest seasonal foods, which have long been the heart of the Mediterranean diet, and the flavor of exotic Morocco. In Moroccan cooking, ras el hanout, meaning "top of the shop", is a commonly used blend of 10–100 spices. Introduced by Kerry Kage Harp Loiacono, this dairy free, gluten free, vegetarian/vegan soup is brought to a new level by a subtle blend of Moroccan spices, coconut milk and lime.

2 Tbsp. olive oil

1 medium onion, diced

3–4 garlic cloves, minced

2 medium carrots, diced

2 celery stalks, diced

2 Tbsp. tomato paste

14 oz. can diced tomatoes

¼ tsp. red pepper flakes

¼ tsp. cayenne pepper

1 tsp. cumin

1 Tbsp. ras el hanout

6 cups vegetable broth

1 cup red lentils, sorted and rinsed

2–14 oz. cans coconut milk

2 Tbsp. cilantro, chopped

¼ tsp. pepper

2 tsp. salt

½ cup lime juice, fresh squeezed

SERVES 6–8

SERVING SUGGESTION:
As garnish, sprinkle 1 teaspoon of roasted pepitas atop the soup.

MOST DIFFICULT

Sauté onions and red pepper flakes in a little olive oil for 5 minutes. Add celery, carrots and garlic; sauté on low heat until vegetables are soft. Add tomato paste, diced tomatoes and a bit of vegetable broth. Simmer 5 minutes.

Add cayenne pepper, cumin and ras el hanout (if unable to locate, substitute with Garam Masal or make your own). Stir. Add remaining vegetable broth and lentils. Boil and reduce heat to simmer for 40 minutes. Stir occasionally.

When lentils are soft, add coconut milk, cilantro, salt and pepper. Simmer for 10 minutes. Add fresh lime juice to soup just before serving.

RAS EL HANOUT

2 Tbsp. Hungarian paprika

1 Tbsp. cumin

1 tsp. cayenne pepper

1 Tbsp. ginger

1 Tbsp. turmeric

1 tsp. nutmeg

1 tsp. cinnamon

1 Tbsp. coriander

1 Tbsp. cardamom

1 Tbsp. chili powder

Mix all ingredients together and store in a jar.

ROASTED PEPITAS

1 cup pumpkin seeds, raw and hulled

1 lime, juiced

Ras el hanout

Cumin

Cayenne pepper

Sea salt

Place pumpkin seeds in a bowl, add lime juice and stir. Add a sprinkle or two of each seasoning and stir. Spread seeds on parchment-lined baking sheet. Bake at 350 degrees for 10–12 minutes, until lightly browned. Cool.

BRAISED ELK & HUCKLEBERRY SOUP

THE ROYAL WOLF • CHEF GLEN CARLSON • DRIGGS, IDAHO

The Royal Wolf in Driggs, Idaho, is the place where locals of Teton Valley socialize! Even though state lines separate The Royal Wolf from Alta, Wyoming's Grand Targhee Resort, they are mere minutes apart. Grand Targhee Resort, a year 'round mountain resort situated on the western slope of the Tetons and located in the Caribou-Targhee National Forest, is continually recognized for its abundance of light powder snow (more than 500 inches annually), genuine western hospitality, scenic beauty, excellent value and commitment to sustainability. The uncrowded lift lines create a paradise for both skiers and snowboarders!

1 lb. elk sirloin

2 oz. dried morel mushrooms

3–4 cups water

2 Tbsp. olive oil, plus some for braising

1 large yellow onion, medium-size chopped

2 Tbsp. garlic, minced

1 Tbsp. black pepper

1 Tbsp. oregano

½ cup flour

1 cup Guinness stout

¼ cup burgundy wine, plus some for braising

2 Tbsp. soy sauce

1 quart + 1 cup beef stock

1 cup pan gravy (or packaged)

1 cup fresh or frozen huckleberries (may use blueberries)

1 cup curly kale, finely chopped, ½-inch shreds

Blue cheese crumbles

1 small potato, cut into fine, short shoestrings (optional)

Salt and pepper to taste

SERVES 4–6

MORE DIFFICULT

Pat elk dry and sprinkle with salt and pepper. You may use beef, lamb or venison if elk isn't available. Other cuts of meat may be used, as well. In a small heavy-bottomed, oven-proof pan, heat braising amount of olive oil and brown meat on all sides. Reduce heat to medium; add braising amount of burgundy wine and 1 cup beef stock to almost cover the meat. Simmer for 5 minutes, then cover pan tightly and place in a 300 degree oven for 45 minutes. Remove elk from braising liquid and save liquid to make gravy or add to soup.

Soak dried morels in lukewarm water for about 30 minutes. Drain and save liquid to add to soup. Chop rehydrated morels into large pieces.

Stirring often, sauté onion in 2 Tbsp. olive oil in a small stock pot until onion is evenly browned. Add garlic, black pepper and oregano; cook until garlic has softened. Add flour and stir until a light golden color. Add Guinness stout and ¼ cup burgundy to deglaze onions and flour. Add chopped morels, soy sauce, 1 quart beef stock and reserved liquid from morels. Simmer until reduced a bit. Add home-made or purchased gravy. Cut elk into 1-inch squares and lightly shred, then add to soup.

Simmer for 20 minutes. While simmering, fry shoestring potatoes until golden. Add all but 2 Tbsp. huckleberries and kale to soup, allowing kale to wilt a bit. Remove soup from heat.

SERVING SUGGESTION:

Garnish each bowl of soup with crispy fried haystack potatoes, blue cheese crumbles and reserved huckleberries.

CREAM OF POTATO SOUP

EATS OF EDEN • EDEN, UTAH

"Eats," as locals refer to Eats of Eden, opened in 1993 and became an instant success with the concept of "simple good food". Of their home-made specialties, the favorite is Cream of Potato Soup, topped with cheese and bacon. This restaurant stays true to its local surroundings by maintaining a rustic outside and a cozy, western-style inside.

8 strips bacon

2 cups cheddar cheese, shredded

2 lbs. potatoes, washed, peeled and cubed

½ cup onions, finely chopped

6 Tbsp. butter

6 Tbsp. flour

3 cups water

1 cup milk

2 cups chicken broth

¼ tsp. garlic, granulated

¼ tsp. ground black pepper

¾ tsp. salt

SERVES 4–6

MORE DIFFICULT

Chop bacon into ½-inch pieces; fry until crispy. Place on a paper towel to drain.

In a large pot, add water, 1 cup chicken broth and potatoes. Boil until potatoes are tender. Drain potatoes and reserve potato water. Set aside.

Melt butter in a large sauce pan. Add onions and cook until softened. Mix in flour. Add 3 cups potato water, milk and remaining chicken broth. Boil and stir until thickened.

Stir in 1 cup cheese. Add garlic, black pepper and salt. Add potatoes and simmer 5 minutes on low. Adjust seasoning.

SERVING SUGGESTION:

Garnish with bacon, remaining cheese, green onions, chives and/or sour cream. Accompany with a great piece of bread.

TOASTED CHICKPEA & SCALLION SOUP

BAR GERNIKA • CHEF SARAH CARRICO • BOISE, IDAHO

Bar Gernika is a Basque Pub and Eatery in Boise, Idaho. Located in the "Cub" building, which was awarded for its historic preservation, Bar Gernika delights patrons with authentic Basque foods, wine and desserts. Basque foods traditionally have French and Spanish flavor profiles. Fittingly, as Bar Gernika is located on The Basque Block, the center of the Basque Community of Boise. Additionally, Bar Gernika won the 3rd Annual Soup TweetUp in 2012, an annual soup-cooking competition which benefits local Boise charities.

4 cans chickpeas, drained and all liquid reserved

3 scallions, bias sliced

1 russet potato, peeled and chopped into 1-inch pieces

1 small carrot, peeled and chopped into 1-inch pieces

3 garlic cloves, peeled and minced

1 medium onion, 1-inch diced

4 cups vegetable broth or stock

3 Tbsp. butter

1 Tbsp. lemon juice

Rice flour

Salt and pepper

Tahini, optional

Sesame seeds, optional

SERVES 6

In a medium saucepan, boil vegetable broth. Add potatoes, carrots, and garlic, along with a pinch of salt. Cook until potatoes begin to break apart. Remove from heat and puree in a blender or with an immersion blender; set aside.

Preheat oven to 500 degrees. In a large bowl, combine drained chickpeas and enough rice flour to lightly coat. Toss together. Spread chickpeas in an even layer on a buttered sheet pan. Bake on top rack of preheated oven, stirring occasionally with a wooden spoon. Once they color, approximately 15–20 minutes, remove from oven and cool.

In a small stock pot, sauté onion in butter, along with a pinch of sugar. Cook on medium-high heat until lightly golden. If necessary, deglaze the pot with a small amount of sherry or chickpea liquid. Stir in the toasted chickpeas. Add remaining chickpea liquid, potato puree and lemon juice. Add scallions and salt and pepper to taste. Add tahini and/or sesame seeds.

SERVING SUGGESTION:
Serve with crusty bread, spread with a small amount of butter and sliced scallions.

WATERMELON GAZPACHO

UPTOWN FARE • PARK CITY, UTAH

The Ski Town Soups marketing team received a lot of input about Uptown Fare and its "amazing", "yummy", "delicious", and "homemade" soups! Uptown Fare was also praised as a place with local personality. And, as Uptown Fare is run by mother-daughter team, Karleen and Nivin Reilly, enjoy a signature soup in a cozy, "family" dining atmosphere.

1 medium watermelon, seedless

½ red onion, diced

2 medium cucumbers, diced

15 oz. can tomato juice

½ cup cilantro, chopped

Salt and pepper to taste

SERVES 4–6

EASIEST

Slice watermelon in half. Cut half of the watermelon into large chunks and place in blender with tomato juice. Blend until juiced. Cut the rest of the watermelon into bite-sized pieces. Place watermelon pieces in a bowl with all ingredients, including watermelon/tomato mixture. Adjust seasoning; if gazpacho is not sweet enough, add a teaspoon of sugar. Chill for several hours to bring out the flavors.

SERVING SUGGESTION:
Serve this refreshing gazpacho chilled.

CHICKEN TARRAGON SOUP

McGRATH'S IRISH PUB • CHEF PATRICK BOANDL • KILLINGTON, VERMONT

Killington Resort stretches across six mountains and features 140 diverse trails served by 22 lifts. Killington's elevation advantage, combined with an extensive 600-acre snowmaking system and 250 inches of annual snowfall, means you'll enjoy the best ski and snowboard conditions every day of the season. Killington, known for its diversity of terrain, provides skiers and riders of all ability levels a choice of wide-open groomed cruisers, narrow classic New England runs, moguls, steeps and trees.

3 lbs. chicken, boneless

1 Tbsp. poultry seasoning

4 Tbsp. vegetable oil

1 large Spanish onion, peeled and diced

3 carrots, peeled and diced

4 celery stalks, diced

2 bay leaves

10 peppercorns

½ cup flour

2 lbs. red potatoes, diced

1 quart chicken stock

1 quart milk

1 cup fresh tarragon, chopped

¼ cup fresh parsley, chopped

Salt and pepper to taste

½ cup cornstarch (optional)

¼ cup cold water (optional)

SERVES 6–8

 MORE DIFFICULT

Place chicken on a sprayed baking sheet. Sprinkle with poultry seasoning, salt and pepper. In a 400 degree oven, roast chicken about 25 minutes or until firm. Dice into small pieces.

In a large stock pot, heat vegetable oil and add onions, carrots, celery, bay leaves and peppercorns. Cook until vegetables are sweated. Add flour and cook for 5 minutes. Stir occasionally. Add potatoes, chicken stock and milk; bring to a boil. Add diced chicken and continue to boil for 30 minutes.

Add fresh tarragon (or ½ cup dried tarragon) and parsley. For a thicker soup, make a slurry with cornstarch and water mixed together; set aside. Lower heat to medium and cook at a low boil for 15 minutes. Before removing soup from stove, add the slurry. Season to taste.

SERVING SUGGESTION:
This soup is flavorful and filling without any embellishments.

CHANTERELLE MUSHROOM SOUP
with Bacon Crisps & Lingonberries

KIMI'S MOUNTAINSIDE BISTRO • SOLITUDE, UTAH

Kimi's Mountainside Bistro, owned by, and named for, restaurateur and culinary expert, Kimi Eklund, was voted Utah's #1 Mountainside Restaurant in 2010 by "Official Best of Utah." Kimi's Mountainside Bistro is a gathering place for foodies. In a relaxed and cozy mountainside setting, inspired by Kimi's travels throughout Europe, the menu reflects Mediterranean, Scandinavian and Western American favorites.

6 slices apple wood-smoked bacon, thick cut

1 lb. fresh, frozen, dried or canned chanterelle mushrooms

4–5 Tbsp. butter

3 shallots, finely diced

3 garlic cloves, minced

1 Tbsp. flour

1 cup port wine

2 cups heavy whipping cream

2 cups beef stock or mushroom broth, low sodium

Pinch of salt

Pinch of cayenne pepper

¼ cup dried lingonberries or cranberries

3 Tbsp. parsley, finely chopped

SERVES 4–6

 MORE DIFFICULT

Cut bacon strips into ½-inch pieces. In a heated non-stick sauté pan, cook bacon for 4–6 minutes or until crispy. Remove bacon from pan and cool on a paper towel-lined plate.

If mushrooms are fresh or dried, wash in a water bath twice to make sure they are very clean. If mushrooms are dried, boil 1 quart of water and pour over dried chanterelles. Rehydrate for 20 minutes or until they are very soft. Drain all mushrooms, whether dried, canned, fresh or frozen. Place ¾ of the chanterelles in a food processor and pulse to small pieces.

In a sauté pan over medium-high heat, melt 3 Tbsp. butter. Add chopped chanterelles, shallots and ⅔ of the minced garlic. Sauté for 8–10 minutes or until chanterelles are tender. Sprinkle with flour and stir until absorbed. Add port wine and simmer until reduced by half, approximately 8–12 minutes. Add cream and stock. Simmer for 25 minutes. Add pinches of seasonings.

Kimi states, "For added flavor, you can add ¼—½ cup of lingonberry preserves to the soup as it is cooking . . . I do that at home all the time and it is fabulous!"

Sauté remaining chanterelles in remaining butter and minced garlic. Season with a pinch of salt.

SERVING SUGGESTION:

Serve the soup warm and top with the sautéed chanterelles, crispy bacon, dried lingonberries or cranberries and sprinkle with fresh parsley. This soup is also great if served with some wonderful Swedish Limpa, rye bread.

SWEET & SPICY ARTICHOKE WITH HAM SOUP

THE PARAMOUNT • STEAMBOAT SPRINGS, COLORADO

Lee and Suzy DeMusis believe an eclectic mix of traditional specialties with a contemporary twist is a perfect fit for a fun and fresh ski town atmosphere! The Sweet and Spicy Artichoke with Ham Soup has simple and fresh ingredients that create the stage to blend traditional favorites with contemporary cuisine. This healthy, wholesome soup can easily be converted to vegan by omitting the ham and garnishing with avocado rather than cheese.

1 sweet potato

2 Tbsp. olive oil, plus more to brush potatoes

Salt

1 habanero pepper, seeded and diced

1 shallot, diced

1 garlic clove, minced

1 Tbsp. fresh thyme, chopped

6 cups chicken or vegan-chicken broth

2 cups fresh or frozen artichoke hearts (not canned)

1 small head cabbage, coarsely chopped

1 cup brown sugar or maple-glazed ham, cooked and chopped

1 Tbsp. cumin

½ Tbsp. coriander

1 Tbsp. black pepper

½ tsp. paprika

SERVES 4–6

 EASIEST

Preheat oven to 400 degrees. Lightly brush sweet potato with olive oil and sprinkle with salt. Pierce small holes in potato, then wrap with foil. Roast for 1 hour. Cool in foil for 30 minutes. Dice sweet potatoes.

Sauté pepper and shallots in 2 Tbsp. olive oil on medium heat, stirring often. Add garlic and thyme; sauté 1 minute. Add remaining ingredients and potatoes. Bring to a simmer and cook about 45 minutes. Stir occasionally. Soup will thicken as it cooks with the potatoes.

SERVING SUGGESTION:

Top with a combination of creamy (cheese, avocado or sour cream), crunchy (nuts, tortilla strips or croutons) and fragrant (green onions, thyme or dill).

BLACK LENTIL SOUP

'RACK SHACK BISCUITS AND BREWS • SOMERS, MONTANA

The 'Rack Shack Biscuits and Brews features culinary items such as this scrumptious soup recipe, made from scratch with a healthy edge!

2 cups black beluga lentils (or green French lentils), picked over and rinsed

1 Tbsp. extra virgin olive oil

1 large onion, chopped

1 garlic clove, minced

1 tsp. salt

14 oz. can crushed tomatoes

14 oz. can fire-roasted diced tomatoes

2 cups water

3 cups spinach, washed and diced

1–2 tsp. smoked paprika, or to taste

SERVES 6–8

 EASIEST In a large pot, bring 6 cups of water to a boil. Add lentils and cook for about 30 minutes, or until tender. Drain and set aside.

Meanwhile, in a heavy pot, heat oil over medium heat. Add onions and salt, sauté until tender. Add garlic and sauté until fragrant, approximately 1 minute. Stir in tomatoes, lentils and water; return to a simmer. Stir in the spinach and smoked paprika.

SERVING SUGGESTION:
This soup is excellent topped with a dollop of sour cream.

VERMONT CURRIED APPLE SOUP

ECHO LAKE INN • CHEF KEVIN BARNES • LUDLOW, VERMONT

Rising above the village of Ludlow in south-central Vermont, Okemo Mountain Resort has built its reputation for quality and superior guest service as a winter retreat for skiers and snowboarders. Originally a small community-run ski hill, Okemo began to blossom in the 1980s after creating "The Okemo Difference". Okemo Mountain Resort consistently earns accolades and awards for snow quality, grooming, terrain parks, family programs, slope side lodging, resort dining and the best guest service in the East.

3 apples, peeled, cored and sliced

1 medium onion, chopped

1 Tbsp. curry powder

2 cups chicken stock

1 cup heavy cream

4 Tbsp. butter

Salt and pepper to taste

SERVES 4

EASIEST

In a heavy sauce pan, sauté onion in melted butter until translucent. Add apples and sauté until they start to soften. Add curry powder and slowly add chicken stock while stirring gently over medium-high heat. Add cream. Simmer for 30 minutes, stirring occasionally.

Season to taste with salt and pepper and additional curry, if desired.

SERVING SUGGESTION:
Serve this soup with a dollop of sour cream.

APPLE & BRIE SOUP

ECHO LAKE INN • CHEF KEVIN BARNES • LUDLOW, VERMONT

For 10 years, Chef Kevin Barnes has been the talented creative force behind the success of the Echo Lake Inn restaurant. His menus reflect the importance of attention to detail, unflagging creativity and the freshest ingredients. With his creative New American Cuisine menu, he introduces well known global choices to allow diners to discover new favorites.

3 Macintosh apples, cored and sliced

8 oz. brie, diced (rind removed)

1 medium onion, diced

4 Tbsp. butter

3 Tbsp. flour

1 cup chicken stock

2 cups heavy cream

Salt and pepper to taste

SERVES 4

Melt butter in heavy sauce pan over medium-high heat. Add diced onion and sauté until translucent. Toss apples lightly with onions until apples soften. Sprinkle flour over mixture and stir until well incorporated. Add salt and pepper to taste.

While stirring, add chicken stock. Slowly, add heavy cream and brie while continuously stirring. Simmer on low heat for about 30 minutes. Stir occasionally. Adjust seasoning.

SERVING SUGGESTION:
Already a perfect pairing, apples and cheese need no additional help.

CREAMY CHICKEN SOUP
with Fregola, Shitakes & Sage

EIGHT K RESTAURANT • CHEF ROB ZACK • SNOWMASS VILLAGE, COLORADO

Around the restaurant fireplace, throughout the dining room, or in the private dining space at the Viceroy Snowmass Eight K Restaurant, lively groups and romantic couples enjoy seasonal menus and classic mountain warmth. Offering fine dining options throughout the day, the restaurant features a glimmering display kitchen at its center and a stunning 87-foot glass bar. Chef Zack, formerly of Eight K, shares a note about this soup—it is best served the next day.

3–4 lbs. whole chicken, skin removed and rinsed

2 cups celery, medium diced

3 cups yellow onions, medium diced

3 cups carrots, medium diced

1 bay leaf

1 Tbsp. fresh thyme, minced

4 quarts chicken stock

1 quart heavy cream

2 cups shitake mushrooms, sliced

2 Tbsp. fresh sage, minced

3 cups fregola or any small pasta, cooked

SERVES 10–12

 MORE DIFFICULT

Boil heavy cream in a 3-quart pot over high heat. Reduce heat to low and simmer until reduced to 2 cups. Cool and reserve in refrigerator for later use.

In a large stock pot, boil chicken and stock over high heat. Simmer with lid ajar. Cook for 30 minutes. Skim any foam that forms on the surface. Add celery, onions, carrots, bay leaf and thyme. Simmer with lid ajar for 30 minutes more. Remove chicken and cool, then remove meat from carcass, pulling into medium-sized pieces. Return carcass to simmering stock. Cover, with lid ajar, and simmer for another 30 minutes. Remove carcass and discard. Add chicken meat back into pot. Season with salt and pepper to taste.

Cool and store overnight in refrigerator.

For final assembly, return soup to a simmer. Add reduced cream and shitakes. Continue to simmer for 5 minutes. Add cooked pasta. Cook until soup is hot and adjust seasoning, if necessary.

SERVING SUGGESTION:
Ladle into warmed bowls and garnish with fresh sage.

GARDEN ZUCCHINI TOMATO BASIL SOUP

CAFÉ REGIS • CHEF LOIDA HARDIN • RED LODGE, MONTANA

In a rocky mountain ski town, such as Red Lodge, Montana, ski-town gardeners can count on frightening amounts of zucchini! Several years ago, Café Regis' Chef Loida Hardin set out on a culinary mission—try to work large quantities of fresh zucchini into the already-celebrated "Nancy's Tomato and Basil Soup" recipe. Garden Zucchini Tomato Basil Soup prevailed and was an instant hit at the café! "We're still big fans of fresh, local produce," says Café Regis owner Martha Young, "even startling eruptions of zucchini."

½ cup onion, diced

1 cup zucchini, sliced length-wise into quarters, then cut vertically into slices

Olive oil

4 cups fresh tomatoes, chopped

½ cup heavy cream

¼ cup fresh basil, chopped

Salt and pepper to taste

SERVES 4–6

Sauté onion and zucchini in a large soup pot with olive oil over medium heat. Add tomatoes (if fresh tomatoes aren't available, use a 28 oz. can diced tomatoes). Simmer for 15 minutes. To reduce the acid in the tomatoes add a pinch of baking soda and ½ tsp. of sugar.

Add heavy cream (for a vegan option, use soy or almond milk). Add fresh basil (or 1 Tbsp. dried basil).

Season with salt and pepper to taste. Simmer for 10 minutes.

SERVING SUGGESTION:

A grilled cheese and avocado sandwich is a perfect complement to this soup.

WORLD FAMOUS ARTICHOKE & CHEDDAR SOUP

THE LAST STEEP BAR AND GRILL • CRESTED BUTTE, COLORADO

Nestled in the heart of Colorado's Rocky Mountains, Crested Butte is committed to preserving the pristine landscape and mountain lifestyle. With vibrant Victorian store fronts and expressive local characters, the small historic town remains true to its heritage radiating an inviting spirit that celebrates a simpler life and time. Thanks to a widely diverse landscape, outdoor enthusiasts of all levels will find a new challenge with each visit. From world-class mountain biking, to legendary skiing and snowboarding, to a secluded fly fishing experience, Crested Butte is one of Colorado's best-kept secrets!

2 carrots, peeled and diced

1 yellow onion, peeled and diced

1 celery bunch, diced

1 tsp. dried thyme leaves

1 tsp. white pepper

4 dashes Tabasco sauce

3 quarts vegetable stock

½ cup butter

½ cup flour

8 oz. cheddarjack cheese, shredded

12 oz. Velveeta cheese, 1-inch cubes

1 quart canned, diced artichoke hearts

SERVES 6–8

 EASIEST

In a large pot, sauté carrots, onions, celery, thyme, white pepper and Tabasco sauce. Sauté until tender. Add vegetable stock and boil.

In a separate pan, melt butter and flour. Stir until incorporated. Slowly add to vegetables to thicken. Simmer and add cheeses while stirring. Add artichokes.

Simmer on low for 10 minutes. Whisk continuously to melt cheeses.

SERVING SUGGESTION:
Serve in a bread bowl topped with shredded cheese and scallions.

MOONLIGHT CHICKEN VERDE

JACK CREEK GRILLE • BIG SKY, MONTANA

Moonlight Basin's Jack Creek Grille is located slope side in the Moonlight Lodge. In this elegant but casual lodge setting, Jack Creek features fine dining selections including mouthwatering grass-fed steaks, creative seafood, wild game and vegetarian dishes, using local and organic products whenever possible.

1 lb. chicken leg and thigh meat

Seasoning mix of salt, black pepper, chili powder, ground cumin and ground coriander

4 Poblano chilies, roasted, steamed, skinned and seeded

3 Tbsp. olive oil

2 onions, diced

2 carrots, diced

4 garlic cloves, minced

2 cups heavy cream

2 quarts chicken stock

1 Tbsp. oregano

2 tsp. cumin

2 Tbsp. coriander

1 bunch cilantro, chopped

1 jalapeno, seeded and chopped

Salt and pepper to taste

SERVES 6–8

Season chicken meat with salt, pepper, chili powder, cumin and coriander. In a 400 degree oven, roast chicken about 25 minutes or until firm. Cool and pull meat apart. In same oven, roast chilies on a baking sheet with a drizzle of olive oil for approximately 30–40 minutes.

In a large stock pot, add 2 Tbsp. olive oil and sauté onions, carrots, garlic and jalapenos until translucent. Add chicken stock and pulled chicken. Simmer for 45 minutes.

Puree seeded and skinned Poblano chilies with heavy cream and chopped cilantro. Add cream and chili mixture to the soup and boil. Season with remaining spices. Adjust seasoning with salt and pepper to taste.

SERVING SUGGESTION:
Enjoy in front of a roaring fire, like you might at the Jack Creek Grille.

ROCKS SHRIMP GAZPACHO

ROCKS MODERN GRILL • AVON, COLORADO

"Chilled soup at a ski resort?" After making fresh tracks on a clear powder day, nothing tastes better. Rocks Shrimp Gazpacho is crisp, incredibly refreshing and full of healthy, light flavors. Chef Mike Spalla, former chef of Rocks Modern Grill, perfected this recipe while working by the beaches; when he moved to the mountains, he realized that it fit the menu and the clientele just as well at altitude, if not better. This recipe was his first televised cooking demo, as he figured the recipe would be quick, easy and simple enough to prepare on camera.

1 lb. rock or cocktail shrimp

30 oz. can crushed tomatoes

2 English cucumbers, skin-on

½ red onion

1 red bell pepper

1 yellow bell pepper

½ small seedless watermelon, chopped

1 small bunch parsley

6 basil leaves, torn by hand into small pieces

½ cup white balsamic or champagne vinegar (or regular balsamic)

2 Tbsp. extra virgin olive oil

Salt and pepper to taste

SERVES 4–6

 EASIEST

Sauté shrimp in 1 Tbsp. olive oil until firm and opaque. Season with salt and pepper to taste, and set aside to cool.

Puree watermelon in a blender until smooth. Add parsley and basil; pulse blender 10 times to chop herbs. Cut cucumbers, onion and peppers into small pieces, about ¼-inch.

In a large bowl, mix all ingredients and season with salt and pepper to taste. Allow gazpacho to rest overnight for flavors to combine. If you can't wait that long, puree ¼ of the soup in a blender and stir back into the mix.

SERVING SUGGESTION:
Enjoy in a chilled martini glass topped with sour cream and fresh lime and surrounded by tortilla chips.

TUSCAN TURKEY & WHITE BEAN SOUP

JOHN HARVARD'S BREW HOUSE • CHEF JOSHUA MCDOWELL • ELLICOTTVILLE, NEW YORK

Chef Joshua McDowell believes this soup is almost an entire meal in itself! It balances wholesome sources of protein and vegetables with the much-needed carbohydrates for any skier. An excellent midday meal!

2½ lbs. turkey, cooked and diced

4 oz. bacon, cooked and diced

¼ cup vegetable oil

2 cups onions, diced

1½ cups celery, diced

1 cup mushrooms, chopped

3 Tbsp. garlic, chopped

3 lbs. great northern beans, cooked

3 lbs. canned diced tomatoes

3 quarts chicken stock

1 lb. fresh spinach, chiffonade

⅛ cup fresh basil, chiffonade

⅛ cup fresh thyme

6 tsp. red wine vinegar

⅛ tsp. cayenne pepper

1 tsp. ground fennel seed

Salt and pepper to taste

SERVES 8–10

MORE DIFFICULT

In a large stock pot, brown turkey in oil. Add onions and celery, sauté until the onions are translucent. Add garlic and sauté until aromatic. Sauté mushrooms in a separate pan. Add beans, mushrooms, stock and tomatoes to turkey mixture. Season with salt and pepper and simmer for 30 minutes.

Add remaining ingredients for final seasoning. But, make sure to add basil, spinach and bacon once the soup is off the burner.

SERVING SUGGESTION:

When made properly, this soup needs no garnish as it has different colors and shapes that make it visually appealing! Merely ladle hot soup into a bowl and enjoy!

ROASTED CORN & VEGETABLE GAZPACHO

RIVERHORSE ON MAIN • CHEF SETH ADAMS • PARK CITY, UTAH

Riverhorse on Main is one of the oldest and most distinguished restaurants on Park City's historic Main Street. In 2000, the Riverhorse received the ultimate honor in the hospitality industry: it was selected by the Forbes Travel Guide (formerly Mobile) as one of the top restaurants in the United States, receiving the Four Star Award. As though being so acknowledged once wasn't enough, Riverhorse has kept this prestigious honor every year since 2000! At the helm for over a decade, Executive Chef and Partner, Seth Adams, offers eclectic seasonal menus with the classic favorites never drifting far away.

3 roasted red bell peppers, peeled, seeded and diced

1 jalapeno, seeded and diced

3 English cucumbers, seeded and diced

1 red onion, diced

5 ears of corn

½ cup flat leaf parsley, chopped

½ cup cilantro, chopped

3 fresh limes, juiced

1½ cups tomato paste

1 gallon vegetable stock

1½ Tbsp. cumin

1½ Tbsp. chili powder

2 Tbsp. salt

¼ tsp. cayenne pepper

SERVES 6–8

 EASIEST

Brush ears of corn with olive oil and season with salt and pepper. Roast in a 425 degree oven for 10 minutes. Cool and cut corn from husk.

Combine stock, tomato paste, lime juice, cumin, chili powder, salt and cayenne. Add all remaining ingredients. Refrigerate for 2–3 hours. Adjust seasoning, according to your taste.

SERVING SUGGESTION:
This simple, fresh summer gazpacho may be elevated by adding fresh crab meat or crab legs.

CORN VELOUTÉ, BLUE POTATO & MUSSELS SOUP

PALMER'S GALLERY BAR & GRILL • CHEF PATRICK HENRY • WHISTLER, BRITISH COLUMBIA

The Whistler Golf Club clubhouse is home to Palmer's Gallery Bar & Grill which overlooks Whistler's surrounding peaks and the 18th green. The restaurant has a wonderful location which is combined with outstanding cuisine and service all in a comfortable atmosphere.

1 large onion

1 small potato

1 leek, white part only

2 celery stalks

2 garlic cloves

6 ears of corn (or about 5 cups canned)

1 cup cream

Salt and pepper to taste

SERVES 4–6

MOST DIFFICULT

Cut kernels off the cob and reserve. Place cobs in a pot and cover with water. Boil and simmer for about 20 minutes. Dice onion, potato, leek and celery. In a stock pot, sweat onions. Add potatoes, leeks and, lastly celery. Mince garlic and add (with most of the corn) to vegetable mixture. When vegetables are cooked, add simmering liquid from cobs until ingredients are covered. Add cream and let rest for 10 minutes. Puree this in a blender or with an immersion blender. Set aside.

POTATO SALAD

4 small blue potatoes

1 shallot

½ lemon, zest and juice

⅓ Tbsp. parsley

2 Tbsp. vegetable oil

Salt and pepper to taste

Dice blue potatoes and blanch. Cool. Finely dice shallot and parsley. Combine these in a mixing bowl with lemon zest, juice and oil. Add potatoes and adjust seasoning.

MUSSELS

2 cups mussels

1 shallot

2 garlic cloves

⅓ Tbsp. thyme

⅓ cup Shramm Vodka

Salt and pepper to taste

Dice shallot, garlic and thyme. In a large skillet, sweat shallot, then add garlic. Deglaze with vodka. Add mussels and thyme until cooked. Cool mussels and remove them from their shells, reserve a few intact for garnish. Season to taste.

HORSERADISH WHIP CREAM

⅓ cup cream

Horseradish to taste

Whip the cream in a standing mixer or with a hand-held mixer. Add fresh or pickled horseradish to taste.

SERVING SUGGESTION:
Assemble Corn Velouté, Potato Salad, Mussels and Horseradish Whip Cream to mirror the adjacent photo.

COLORADO BAKED POTATO AVALANCHE SOUP

ROCKS MODERN GRILL • AVON, COLORADO

Enter Beaver Creek Resort through the welcome gate and find a secluded village in an intimate mountain setting that offers, arguably, the best guest service in the world—with the promise of "Not Exactly Roughing It." Explore three unique mountain experiences with European style village-to-village skiing. After a great day on the mountain, enjoy the favorite soup of Chef Mike Spalla, former chef of Rocks Modern Grill: Colorado Baked Potato Avalanche Soup. Creamy, smooth and smoky, it's an old family recipe, passed down over the generations and embellished by Chef Spalla, while still receiving mom's approval. He loves the way the tangy notes of the goat cheese play off the mellow earthiness of the potatoes. Comfort food at its most elegant!

4 Rio Grande potatoes, baker's size

2 tsp. extra virgin olive oil

6 strips apple wood-smoked bacon, cooked crisp, crumbled; reserve the fat

2 Tbsp. butter

1 white onion, diced

1 carrot, peeled and diced

1 small head broccoli

3 cups low-sodium chicken stock

3 cups half and half

½ cup dry white wine, such as Chardonnay

1 small bunch chives, ½-inch pieces

4 oz. Avalanche Garlic and Basil Chevre Goat Cheese, plus more for garnish

1 cup smoked Gouda or cheddar, shredded

2 tsp. Captain Spongefoot Hot Sauce

2 tsp. Worcestershire sauce

Salt and pepper to taste

Sour cream, for garnish

SERVES 4–6

MORE DIFFICULT

Scrub potatoes clean and pat dry. Rub with olive oil and liberal amounts of salt and pepper. Place potatoes on a small sheet pan and bake at 350 degrees for 45 minutes or until easily pierced with a knife. Allow to cool completely at room temperature, about 1½ hours. Cut into 1-inch chunks leaving the skins attached.

Cut the broccoli into small florets. Sauté onions and carrots in butter and reserved bacon fat in a large stock pot until soft. Add wine and half of the crumbled bacon; bring to a boil. Add chicken stock, half and half, cheeses, broccoli and half of the potatoes. Boil and reduce to a simmer. Allow to cook for 15 minutes, stirring occasionally to prevent cheese from sticking to the bottom of the pot.

Puree soup with a blending wand or in a blender. Return to pot. Simmer, and add the rest of the potatoes, hot sauce and Worcestershire, and season with salt and pepper to taste.

SERVING SUGGESTION:
Best served steaming out of a mug, late in the afternoon on a crisp winter day—sore feet elevated towards the mountain that was just conquered. Garnish with sour cream, chives, the remaining bacon and more Avalanche goat cheese.

LOCAL FRENCH ONION SOUP

CACHE CACHE BISTRO • CHEF CHRIS LANTER • ASPEN, COLORADO

This recipe has been rated "Most Difficult" for the pure fact of time: cooking time for veal demi-glace can be 2–3 days. A home cook may not attempt to make this due to the long cooking time, but it is well worth an executive chef's while. Cache Cache Bistro is a fine dining restaurant which includes French and Provencal cuisine and a great vegetarian selection.

2½ Tbsp. blended oil (75% canola, 25% extra virgin olive oil)

3 Tbsp. unsalted butter

3 lbs. sweet yellow onions, sliced

4–5 cups brandy

1 quart chicken stock

2 cups veal demi-glace, home-made or store-bought

1 Tbsp. Herbes de Provence

Kosher salt and ground black pepper

3 cups Gruyère cheese, grated

1 "Louis Swiss" baguette

SERVES 6

In a roasting pan, melt butter and oil together. When very hot, add onions. Caramelize onions, stirring occasionally. Carefully add brandy and reduce by half on medium heat. Add chicken stock and veal demi-glace. If using store-bought veal demi-glace, purchase (2) 1-cup packets. Bring to a simmer, and let it cook for 20–30 minutes so the flavors develop.

Finish soup with herbs and season to taste.

SERVING SUGGESTION:

Ladle soup into six oven-proof bowls and place two ½-inch sliced, lightly toasted baguettes atop soup. Distribute ½ cup Gruyère evenly atop baguette slices. Place under the broiler and toast until golden brown.

REUBEN SOUP

BUFFALO GAL • CHEF TOM STEINBERG • DONNELLY, IDAHO

Casual-dining establishment, Buffalo Gal, features contemporary cuisine just minutes from Tamarack Resort. Therefore, it's not surprising that when Chef Tom Steinberg is not in the kitchen creating unique recipes like Reuben Soup, he can be found skiing through the trees in feet-deep powder.

1 yellow onion, diced

2 carrots, diced

1 lb. corned beef or pastrami, cut into ¼-inch cubes

1 small green cabbage, julienned

2 Tbsp. garlic, chopped

1 Tbsp. caraway seeds

1½ tsp. black pepper

1 Tbsp. marjoram

1 Tbsp. Dijon mustard

¼ cup clarified butter

¼ cup flour

12 oz. beer

3 quarts chicken stock

6 oz. Swiss cheese, grated

Tabasco sauce to taste

Salt and pepper to taste

SERVES 6–8

MORE DIFFICULT

In a thick bottomed stock pot, heat 2 Tbsp. clarified butter. Add onions and carrots, sauté until soft. Add cabbage and sauté until soft. Add garlic, pepper, caraway seeds, marjoram and remaining clarified butter, sauté until aromatic.

Reduce to low heat, stir in flour, cook for 2–3 minutes. Add Swiss cheese and mustard; stir until cheese is fully incorporated. Add beer and cook off alcohol for 2–3 minutes. Add chicken stock and meat. Bring to a simmer over low heat, stirring frequently (otherwise, it can easily stick to the pot and burn).

Add salt, pepper and Tabasco to taste.

SERVING SUGGESTION:
As you would expect, rye bread makes a great accompaniment to this soup.

Rogan Lechthaler

Chef Rogan Lechthaler is as creative in the kitchen as he is adept on skis! Over 12 years, the Weston, Vermont, native has honed his eclectic culinary skills everywhere from Boston to Mississippi; he now specializes in using local, seasonal ingredients in Vermont.

Chef Rogan started his career in 1999 at The Ritz Carlton in Boston, before moving to Mistral, a see-and-be-seen restaurant in Boston's South End. In 2004, he returned to the Green Mountains with a position at Warren's Relais & Châteaux Pitcher Inn. Around this time, he began wooing his Mississippi-bred wife, and now business partner, Abby Lechthaler, and later left for culinary positions at Blackberry Farm in Walland, TN, Bayona in New Orleans, LS, then L&M's Salumeria in Oxford, MS. Beckoned back to Vermont in 2007, Chef Lechthaler became Head Chef at Stratton Mountain's Verdé.

In November 2010, the Lechthalers bought The Downtown Grocery (formerly Cappuccino's) near Okemo Mountain in Ludlow, Vermont. Chef Rogan makes his own pastas, sources fresh, sustainable seafood and cures his own meats in the cellar beneath his casual fine dining eatery. His seasonal, regional cooking has been featured in Outside magazine, Burlington's SEVEN DAYS, and on Boston's NBC affiliate. In March 2010, he was selected to cook with five other top Vermont chefs at New York's James Beard House.

See page 125 for Chef Rogan Lechthaler's Wild Maine Shrimp Gumbo.

Clark Church

Clark Church, former Chef and Owner of Garnish Restaurant & Catering in Aspen / Snowmass, is famous in the area for his soups! Every January, Aspen hosts the Soupsköl Competition, a soup-cooking contest judged by the public to determine which local establishment has the best soup in town. Clark won the competition in 2007, 2008 and 2009 for his well-known Church's Chowder (New England Clam Chowder) and kept his title in 2010 for a new soup, his Wisconsin Beer Cheese Soup. Church's Chowder was also recognized in *Aspen* Magazine's Summer 2009 Bucket List as one of the 87 "Feel Good Things to Eat Before You Die."

Garnish Restaurant & Catering was established in 2007 after Clark worked for four years as the Sous Chef at the famous Hotel Jerome in Aspen. Before that, he was the Executive Chef at the Whitetail Inn, a fine dining establishment in Northern Wisconsin. Chef Church has relocated to Parker, Colorado, as Executive Chef of the Pinery Country Club.

See page 96 for Chef Clark Church's Chowder.

Gavin McMichael

Before opening The Blacksmith in Downtown Bend, Oregon, Chef Gavin McMichael was Executive Chef at a handful of high-profile guest ranches and upscale restaurants. He previously served as Executive Sous-Chef for Stephen Pyles on his television show, New Tastes of Texas. McMichael has also worked as Executive Chef to the rich and famous on exclusive charter yachts in the Mediterranean, Caribbean and Pacific Northwest. The Blacksmith has been recognized by Conde Nast Traveler as one of the "top 66 new restaurants in the world."

Serving distinctive New Ranch Cuisine, The Blacksmith upgrades American comfort food to a sophisticated status. The restaurant fuses old and new, perfectly complementing Texan Chef Gavin McMichael's urban cowboy-inspired cuisine, creating new classics like "Lobster Corndogs," "Not Your Mother's Meatloaf," and "Northwest Cheese Steak."

"There is not much New Ranch style cooking being done in this area, but I think this cuisine makes a lot of sense. Central Oregon is cowboy country in a lot of respects, and I knew there was a good chance it would be very well received," said Chef Gavin McMichael. "Oregon has such a great frontier history and bounty of ingredients that it's easy for a chef to embrace."

See page 56 for Chef Gavin McMichael's Smoked Tomato Bisque with Grilled Cheese Dipper.

See page 139 for Chef Gavin McMichael's Smoked Brisket Chili.

Photography Credits

John Wiese, Wiese Photo

Kevin Johnston, Johnston Imaging

Sharon Brezina, Brezina Design

Francis Faillace, Pure Mint Media

Shea Evans Photography

Matt Power, Matt Power Photography

Ken Redding Photography

Corey Hendrickson

Chuck Halsey

Denise Gelineau

John James Sherlock, John Sherlock Studio

Dan Harper, DSH Photography

Andrew Rupczynski, Andrew Rupczynski Photography

Jeff Scroggins Photography

Jude Rubadue

McKenzie McDonald Christensen

Tamika Garscia Photography

Peak Photography

Tripp Fay, Tripp Fay Photography

Jack Affleck, Jack Affleck Photography

Cody Downard, Cody Downard

Dan Davis

Seth Bullington

Aaron Dodds

Carl Scofield

Bob Winsett

Leisa Gibson

Brian Bailey

TJ Greenwood

Spencer Leonard

Chris McLennan

Tom Green

Corey Rich

Joseph Keum

Mt Bachelor

Stratton Mountain Resort

Heavenly Mountain Resort

Okemo Mountain Resort

Beaver Creek Resort

Grand Targhee Resort

Telluride Ski Resort

Snowbasin: A Sun Valley Resort

Whiteface Mountain

Taos Ski Valley

Big Sky Resort

Omni Mount Washington Resort

Park City Mountain Resort

Copper Mountain Resort

Stowe Mountain Resort

Smugglers' Notch Resort, Vermont

Whitefish Mountain Resort

Aspen Chamber of Commerce

Deer Valley Resort

Snowbird Ski Resort

Sugarbush Resort

Professional Acknowledgements

This cookbook would not have been possible without the help of many resourceful souls! I appreciate the generosity and timely responses from all restaurants and ski resorts, which included recipes, write-ups and photos! I would like to thank the concierges, travelers, chambers of commerce and any other points of contact during our initial voting process—your comments and candid feedback were essential in determining the restaurants included in this book.

An especially big thank you to Sarah John and Kelly Liken from Restaurant Kelly Liken—you both assisted with the foreword for this book, as well as providing beautiful photos and a scrumptious soup recipe. Yas Bakshian, thank you for your initial design assistance and marketing collateral that gave a stellar first impression! Thank you, Janine Heffelfinger and Dorie McClelland, for your professional recommendations. Jan Apple, thank you for your extremely giving nature; I absolutely appreciate your keen senses, eagle-eye, and meticulous observations! Bruce Pettit, thank you for your printing expertise and knowledge. *Ski Town Soups* has received many positive comments regarding the website and blog, so thank you Dan Gustafson for your design and creativity. Kevin Johnston, thank you for the photo retouching that you so expertly provided. Susan Kroese and John Wiese, thank you for your "hand-holding" through the food styling, art direction and photography for many of the soups. Your wisdom and creativity were enormously comforting and provided very rewarding results! Finally, I want to thank Jay Monroe from James Monroe Design! You have provided a nurturing, supportive and incredibly artistic avenue for the book design process. Your relaxed personality eased me through uncharted waters, so thank you!

Personal Dedications

I would like to give personal thanks to my book club girls and friends: thank you for making soups to test and photograph, Erin Omann, Sue Clifford, Diane Crater, Rachel Kaul, Donna Dalton, Stacy Tepp, Trudy Berggren and Daria Berger. Most especially, I would like to thank Amy Simpson, Mari Bern, Kjerstin Ohnstad, Melinda Carlson, Kristy Campbell and Jill Redmond for making soups for the photo shoot and supporting this project with genuine excitement! I really could not have done this without your "gourmet night" inspiration and your setting of high standards, whether through motherhood, friendship or professional careers. A special thanks to Kristy Campbell for your fine-toothed comb and attention to details of the English language! To all my friends, I am humbled by your generosity!

I thank my family members, especially my grandmother, Mary (Twink) Robbins and both my mothers, Denise Lassey and Pam Iverson. You've not only made soups and lent bowls, but you've encouraged this project with pats on the back and help around the house! Thank you, also, Pam Iverson, for assisting my soup obsession with a jump-start soup cooking class instructed by the original soup queen, Meredith Deeds, at Cooks on Crocus Hill. From the day of that cooking class until the present, my husband has begged me to find another culinary fixation besides soup, as he's had all types, even a raspberry dessert soup with brownie croutons!

The most important dedication is to Ross, my husband, business partner, confidante, best friend and loving beacon of motivation and encouragement. You have been utterly and amazingly supportive and thoughtful through this seemingly never-ending process. Daily, you impress me with your calm, cool and collected nature, while understanding that I possess not an ounce of these traits. I am astounded that *Ski Town Soups* started as a thought—a dream really—of merging our passions: soup/restaurant eating, traveling and skiing. The idea transformed into reality during our weekly Monday meetings (thank you, Mel and Allie Fiedler, for making these possible). A very insightful saying states, "If you want something done, ask a busy person to do it. The more things you do, the more you can do." That would be you—you continually power through and get it done! Thank you for fitting *Ski Town Soups* and Ski Town Group into your professional life and letting it trickle over to our personal life!

Finally, to my two sons, Love Bug and Prince Munchkin, thank you for drinking pureed soup through straws and being "adventurous" with each meal! Because of you, Grant and Hunter, I am stronger and more inspired each day. My motivation is to make you both proud, and to always be there for you after a day on the mountain!

INDEX

About the Author

Jennie Iverson is the author of the *Ski Town Soups* cookbook, which features signature soups from world class ski resorts. She is also a wife and a mother of two rambunctious boys, all of whom savor days on the mountain. Not only does she love the snow, but she has a general adoration of winter! She's totally enthusiastic about making soups, stews and chilies in cold weather, and relishing a bowl in front of the fire with her family.

Three years ago, she started a journey to hunt down the best soups as she traveled to Sun Valley, Jackson Hole, Mt. Bachelor, Mt. Hood, Whitefish Mountain, Big Sky, Moonlight Basin, Heavenly, Northstar, Park City, Vail and Beaver Creek. What has grown from these travel experiences has been a perfectly balanced recipe for life: a ski town, a comfortable restaurant and a yummy bowl of soup. Reaffirming that, although soup is typically meant to simmer, life is meant to boil!